S0-AYS-715

A Gift For:

_____Matt_____

From:

_____Mom & Dad_____

My son, do not forget my teaching,

    but keep my commands in your heart,

for they will prolong your life many years

    and bring you prosperity.

PROVERBS 3:1–2

ZONDERVAN®

Promises for Men: from the New International Version
Copyright © 2006 by The Zondervan Corporation

Requests for information should be addressed to:
Zondervan, *Grand Rapids, Michigan 49530*

ISBN-10: 0-310-81007-8
ISBN-13: 978-0-310-81007-0

All Scripture quotations, unless otherwise noted, are taken from the *Holy Bible: New International Version*, (North American Edition)®. Copyright © 1973, 1978, 1984, by International Bible Society. Used by permission of Zondervan Publishing House. All rights reserved.

The "NIV" and "New International Version" trademarks are registered in the United States Patent and Trademark Office by International Bible Society.

All rights reserved. No part of this publication may be reproduced, stored in a retrieval system, or transmitted in any form or by any means — electronic, mechanical, photocopy, recording, or any other — except for brief quotations in printed reviews, without the prior permission of the publisher.

Printed in the United States of America

08 09 10 11 12 • 15 14 13 12 11 10 9 8 7 6 5 4 3

Promises
for Men

from the New International Version

ZONDERVAN®

INTRODUCTION

*The great and glorious promises of God—
they are our security in a world of uncertainty
and turmoil. They are life vests, intended to
protect us through stormy seas. They are
God's gifts given corporately to all of his children—but personally to each one of us.*

*We've compiled this book, Promises for
Men, so that you can take hold of God's
promises for your life. We pray that as you
read, you will begin to understand how vast
his promises really are, covering virtually
every area of daily life. Then, it's our hope
that you will appropriate them as God
intended, whether your skies are sunny or
gray, both in good times and bad. God's
promises are sufficient to cover any need you
might have.*

So read them, believe them, rely on them, treasure them. Most of all, thank God for them. Though freely given, they have been bought with a great price—the holy, righteous blood of God's precious son, Jesus.

For the sake of your servant and according to your will, you have done this great thing and made known all these great promises.

1 CHRONICLES 17:19

TABLE OF CONTENTS

God's promises are *like the* stars; the darker *the* night the brighter *they* shine.

DAVID NICHOLAS

ACCEPTANCE

God said, "You are my servant;
  I have chosen you and have not rejected you."

ISAIAH 41:9

Accept one another, then, just as Christ accepted you, in order to bring praise to God.

ROMANS 15:7

There is neither Jew nor Greek, slave nor free, male nor female, for you are all one in Christ Jesus.

GALATIANS 3:28

Jesus said, "All that the Father gives me will come to me, and whoever comes to me I will never drive away."

JOHN 6:37

How good and pleasant it is
  when brothers live together in unity!

PSALM 133:1

Jesus said, "He who receives you receives me, and he who receives me receives the one who sent me."

MATTHEW 10:40

Jesus said, "Give to the one who asks you, and do not turn away from the one who wants to borrow from you. You have heard that it was said, 'Love your neighbor and hate your enemy.' But I tell you: Love your enemies and pray for those who persecute you."

MATTHEW 5:42–44

To love [God] with all your heart, with all your understanding and with all your strength, and to love your neighbor as yourself is more important than all burnt offerings and sacrifices.

MARK 12:33

For the sake of his great name the LORD will not reject his people, because the LORD was pleased to make you his own.

1 SAMUEL 12:22

Praise be to the God and Father of our Lord Jesus Christ. . . . He chose us in him before the creation of the world to be holy and blameless in his sight. In love he predestined us to be adopted as his sons through Jesus Christ, in accordance with his pleasure and will.

EPHESIANS 1:3–5

ACCOMPLISHMENT

LORD, you establish peace for us;
    all that we have accomplished you
        have done for us.

ISAIAH 26:12

*"Not by might nor by power, but by my Spirit," says
the LORD Almighty.*

ZECHARIAH 4:6

A longing fulfilled is a tree of life.

PROVERBS 13:12

*Whatever was to my profit I now consider loss for
the sake of Christ. What is more, I consider everything a loss compared to the surpassing greatness of
knowing Christ Jesus my Lord, for whose sake I
have lost all things. I consider them rubbish, that I
may gain Christ and be found in him, not having a
righteousness of my own that comes from the law,
but that which is through faith in Christ—the righteousness that comes from God and is by faith.*

PHILIPPIANS 3:7–9

The plans of the LORD stand firm forever,
the purposes of his heart through all
generations.

PSALM 33:11

With [God's] help I can advance
against a troop;
with my God I can scale a wall.

PSALM 18:29

I have fought the good fight, I have finished the
race, I have kept the faith. Now there is in store for
me the crown of righteousness, which the Lord, the
righteous Judge, will award to me on that day—
and not only to me, but also to all who have longed
for his appearing.

2 TIMOTHY 4:7–8

Commit to the LORD whatever
you do,
and your plans will succeed.

PROVERBS 16:3

ADVICE & COUNSEL

Wisdom is found in those who take advice.

PROVERBS 13:10

This is what the LORD *says:*
"Stand at the crossroads and look;
ask for the ancient paths,
ask where the good way is, and walk in it,
and you will find rest for your souls."

JEREMIAH 6:16

The LORD *says, "Call to me and I will answer you*
and tell you great and unsearchable things you do
not know."

JEREMIAH 33:3

I will praise the LORD*, who counsels me;*
even at night my heart instructs me.

PSALM 16:7

Plans fail for lack of counsel, but with many advisers they succeed.

PROVERBS 15:22

Jesus said, "The Counselor, the Holy Spirit, whom the Father will send in my name, will teach you all things and will remind you of everything I have said to you."

JOHN 14:26

To God belong wisdom and power;
    counsel and understanding are his.

JOB 12:13

I will instruct you and teach you in the way you
        should go;
    I will counsel you and watch over you.

PSALM 32:8

The way of a fool seems right to him,
    but a wise man listens to advice.

PROVERBS 12:15

Listen to advice and accept instruction,
    and in the end you will be wise.

PROVERBS 19:20

AMBITION

Aim for perfection, listen to my appeal, be of one mind, live in peace. And the God of love and peace will be with you.

2 CORINTHIANS 13:11

In his heart a man plans his course,
but the LORD determines his steps.

PROVERBS 16:9

May [the LORD] give you the desire of your heart
and make all your plans succeed.

PSALM 20:4

Make it your ambition to lead a quiet life, to mind
your own business and to work with your hands,
just as we told you, so that your daily life may win
the respect of outsiders and so that you will not be
dependent on anybody.

1 THESSALONIANS 4:11–12

Delight yourself in the LORD
and he will give you the desires of your heart.

PSALM 37:4

Christ's love compels us, because we are convinced that one died for all, and therefore all died. And he died for all, that those who live should no longer live for themselves but for him who died for them and was raised again.

2 CORINTHIANS 5:14–15

Make plans by seeking advice.

PROVERBS 20:18

Be all the more eager to make your calling and election sure. For if you do these things, you will never fall, and you will receive a rich welcome into the eternal kingdom of our Lord and Savior Jesus Christ.

2 PETER 1:10–11

*Many are the plans in a man's heart,
    but it is the LORD's purpose that prevails.*

PROVERBS 19:21

The desires of the diligent are fully satisfied.

PROVERBS 13:4

ANSWERED PRAYER

*Jesus said, "In that day you will no longer ask me
anything. I tell you the truth, my Father will give
you whatever you ask in my name. Until now you
have not asked for anything in my name. Ask and
you will receive, and your joy will be complete."*

JOHN 16:23–24

*"They will not toil in vain
      or bear children doomed to misfortune;
for they will be a people blessed by the LORD,
      they and their descendants with them.
Before they call I will answer;
      while they are still speaking I will hear,"
            says the LORD.*

ISAIAH 65:23–24

[God] does not ignore the cry of
      the afflicted.

PSALM 9:12

*In my distress I called to the LORD,
      and he answered me.
From the depths of the grave I called for help,
      and you listened to my cry.*

JONAH 2:2

The LORD has heard my weeping.
The LORD has heard my cry for mercy;
the LORD accepts my prayer.

PSALM 6:8–9

This is the confidence we have in approaching God:
that if we ask anything according to his will, he
hears us. And if we know that he hears us—what-
ever we ask—we know that we have what we asked
of him.

1 JOHN 5:14–15

Jesus said, "Ask and it will be given to you; seek
and you will find; knock and the door will be
opened to you. For everyone who asks receives; he
who seeks finds; and to him who knocks, the door
will be opened."

MATTHEW 7:7–8

[God] will respond to the prayer of the destitute;
he will not despise their plea.
Let this be written for a future generation,
that a people not yet created may praise
the LORD.

PSALM 102:17–18

The LORD is near to all who call on him,
    to all who call on him in truth.
He fulfills the desires of those who fear him;
    he hears their cry and saves them.

PSALM 145:18–19

Jesus said, "Whatever you ask for in prayer, believe that you have received it, and it will be yours."

MARK 11:24

"Call upon me in the day of trouble;
    I will deliver you, and you will honor me,"
        declares the LORD.

PSALM 50:15

Cast your cares on the LORD
and he will sustain you;
he will never let the righteous fall.

PSALM 55:22

Jesus said, "Again, I tell you that if two of you on earth agree about anything you ask for, it will be done for you by my Father in heaven."

MATTHEW 18:19

Jesus said, "If you believe, you will receive whatever you ask for in prayer."

MATTHEW 21:22

Now I know that the LORD saves his anointed;
   he answers him from his holy heaven
   with the saving power of his right hand.

PSALM 20:6

To the LORD I cry aloud,
and he answers me from his
holy hill.

PSALM 3:4

I call on you, O God, for you will answer me;
   give ear to me and hear my prayer.

PSALM 17:6

Jesus said, "I will do whatever you ask in my name,
so that the Son may bring glory to the Father. You
may ask me for anything in my name, and I will
do it."

JOHN 14:13–14

ASSURANCE

It is God who makes both us and you stand firm in Christ. He anointed us, set his seal of ownership on us, and put his Spirit in our hearts as a deposit, guaranteeing what is to come.

2 CORINTHIANS 1:21–22

Jesus said, "I give [my sheep] eternal life, and they shall never perish; no one can snatch them out of my hand. My Father, who has given them to me, is greater than all; no one can snatch them out of my Father's hand."

JOHN 10:28–29

We are more than conquerors through him who loved us.

ROMANS 8:37

Jesus said, "I tell you the truth, whoever hears my word and believes him who sent me has eternal life and will not be condemned; he has crossed over from death to life."

JOHN 5:24

Those who have served well gain an excellent standing and great assurance in their faith in Christ Jesus.

1 TIMOTHY 3:13

*"Though the mountains be shaken
    and the hills be removed,
yet my unfailing love for you will not be shaken
    nor my covenant of peace be removed,"
    says the LORD, who has compassion on you.*

ISAIAH 54:10

*Since we have confidence to enter the Most Holy
Place by the blood of Jesus ... let us draw near to
God with a sincere heart in full assurance of faith,
having our hearts sprinkled to cleanse us from a
guilty conscience and having our bodies washed with
pure water.*

HEBREWS 10:19, 22

*As high as the heavens are above the earth,
    so great is his love for those who fear him;
as far as the east is from the west,
    so far has he removed our transgressions
        from us.*

PSALM 103:11–12

*I know whom I have believed, and am convinced
that he is able to guard what I have entrusted to him
for that day.*

2 TIMOTHY 1:12

God is our God for ever and ever; he will be our guide even to the end.

PSALM 48:14

I am convinced that neither death nor life, neither angels nor demons, neither the present nor the future, nor any powers, neither height nor depth, nor anything else in all creation, will be able to separate us from the love of God that is in Christ Jesus our Lord.

ROMANS 8:38–39

This is what the LORD says to you: "Do not be afraid or discouraged.... For the battle is not yours, but God's."

2 CHRONICLES 20:15

We want each of you to show this same diligence to the very end, in order to make your hope sure. We do not want you to become lazy, but to imitate those who through faith and patience inherit what has been promised.

HEBREWS 6:11–12

Jesus declared, "All that the Father gives me will come to me, and whoever comes to me I will never drive away. For I have come down from heaven not to do my will but to do the will of him who sent me. And this is the will of him who sent me, that I shall lose none of all that he has given me, but raise them up at the last day."

JOHN 6:37–39

I am the LORD, your God,
    who takes hold of your right hand
and says to you, Do not fear;
    I will help you.

ISAIAH 41:13

If our hearts do not condemn us, we have confidence before God and receive from him anything we ask.

1 JOHN 3:21–22

*The ordinances of the LORD are sure
    and altogether righteous.
They are more precious than gold.*

PSALM 19:9–10

ATTITUDE

Whoever claims to live in [God] must walk as Jesus did.

1 JOHN 2:6

Your attitude should be the same as that of
Christ Jesus:
Who, being in very nature God,
did not consider equality with God something to
be grasped,
but made himself nothing,
taking the very nature of a servant,
being made in human likeness.
And being found in appearance as a man,
he humbled himself
and became obedient to death—
even death on a cross!
Therefore God exalted him to the highest place
and gave him the name that is above every name.

PHILIPPIANS 2:5–9

What does the LORD *require of you?*
To act justly and to love mercy
and to walk humbly with your God.

MICAH 6:8

Put off your old self, which is being corrupted by its deceitful desires; to be made new in the attitude of your minds; and to put on the new self, created to be like God in true righteousness and holiness.

EPHESIANS 4:22–24

Guard your heart,
for it is the wellspring of life.

PROVERBS 4:23

Jesus said, "The greatest among you will be your servant. For whoever exalts himself will be humbled, and whoever humbles himself will be exalted."

MATTHEW 23:11–12

Since, then, you have been raised with Christ, set your hearts on things above, where Christ is seated at the right hand of God. Set your minds on things above, not on earthly things.

COLOSSIANS 3:1–2

Be imitators of God, therefore, as dearly loved children and live a life of love, just as Christ loved us and gave himself up for us as a fragrant offering and sacrifice to God.

EPHESIANS 5:1–2

BELIEF

To all who received [Jesus], to those who believed in his name, he gave the right to become children of God—children born not of natural descent, nor of human decision or a husband's will, but born of God.

JOHN 1:12–13

Believe in the Lord Jesus, and you will be saved—you and your household.

ACTS 16:31

Jesus said, "Whoever believes in me is not condemned."

JOHN 3:18

If you confess with your mouth, "Jesus is Lord," and believe in your heart that God raised him from the dead, you will be saved. For it is with your heart that you believe and are justified, and it is with your mouth that you confess and are saved.

ROMANS 10:9–10

Jesus said, "God so loved the world that he gave his one and only Son, that whoever believes in him shall not perish but have eternal life."

JOHN 3:16

All the prophets testify about him that everyone who believes in him receives forgiveness of sins through his name.

ACTS 10:43

Jesus told him, "Because you have seen me, you have believed; blessed are those who have not seen and yet have believed."

JOHN 20:29

Without faith it is impossible to please God, because anyone who comes to him must believe that he exists and that he rewards those who earnestly seek him.

HEBREWS 11:6

Though you have not seen [Jesus Christ], you love him; and even though you do not see him now, you believe in him and are filled with an inexpressible and glorious joy, for you are receiving the goal of your faith, the salvation of your souls.

1 PETER 1:8–9

Jesus said, "I tell you the truth, he who believes has everlasting life."

JOHN 6:47

*On the last and greatest day of the Feast, Jesus stood
and said in a loud voice, "If anyone is thirsty, let
him come to me and drink. Whoever believes in me,
as the Scripture has said, streams of living water will
flow from within him."*

JOHN 7:37–38

See, I lay a stone in Zion,
   a chosen and precious
      cornerstone,
and the one who trusts in him
   will never be put to shame.

I PETER 2:6

*Jesus said to her, "I am the resurrection and the life.
He who believes in me will live, even though he dies;
and whoever lives and believes in me will never die."*

JOHN 11:25–26

*Jesus cried out, "When a man believes in me, he
does not believe in me only, but in the one who sent
me. When he looks at me, he sees the one who sent
me. I have come into the world as a light, so that no
one who believes in me should stay in darkness."*

JOHN 12:44–46

From the beginning God chose you to be saved through the sanctifying work of the Spirit and through belief in the truth. He called you to this through our gospel, that you might share in the glory of our Lord Jesus Christ.

2 THESSALONIANS 2:13–14

It is written, "I believed; therefore I have spoken." With that same spirit of faith we also believe and therefore speak, because we know that the one who raised the Lord Jesus from the dead will also raise us with Jesus and present us with you in his presence.

2 CORINTHIANS 4:13–14

Jesus said, "Everything is possible for him who believes."

MARK 9:23

I am not ashamed, because I know whom I have believed, and am convinced that he is able to guard what I have entrusted to him for that day.

2 TIMOTHY 1:12

BIBLE STUDY

My son, if you accept my words
    and store up my commands within you,
turning your ear to wisdom
    and applying your heart to understanding,
and if you call out for insight
    and cry aloud for understanding,
then you will understand the fear of the LORD
    and find the knowledge of God.
For the LORD gives wisdom,
    and from his mouth come knowledge
        and understanding.

PROVERBS 2:1–3, 5–6

Do your best to present yourself to God as one approved, a workman who does not need to be ashamed and who correctly handles the word of truth.

2 TIMOTHY 2:15

We have the word of the prophets made more certain, and you will do well to pay attention to it, as to a light shining in a dark place, until the day dawns and the morning star rises in your hearts.

2 PETER 1:19

I have hidden your word in my heart
that I might not sin against you.

PSALM 119:11

*The man who looks intently into the perfect law
that gives freedom, and continues to do this, not
forgetting what he has heard, but doing it—he will
be blessed in what he does.*

JAMES 1:25

When your words came, I ate them;
they were my joy and my heart's
delight.

JEREMIAH 15:16

*Jesus answered, "It is written: 'Man does not live on
bread alone, but on every word that comes from the
mouth of God.'"*

MATTHEW 4:4

*Jesus said to them, "Others, like seed sown on good
soil, hear the word, accept it, and produce a crop—
thirty, sixty or even a hundred times what was sown."*

MARK 4:20

BLESSINGS

Blessings crown the head of the righteous.

PROVERBS 10:6

Praise be to the God and Father of our Lord Jesus Christ, who has blessed us in the heavenly realms with every spiritual blessing in Christ.

EPHESIANS 1:3

Blessed is he who comes in the
name of the LORD.
From the house of the LORD we
bless you.

PSALM 118:26

There is no difference between Jew and Gentile— the same Lord is Lord of all and richly blesses all who call on him.

ROMANS 10:12

*Blessed are those you choose
and bring near to live in your courts!
We are filled with the good things of your house,
of your holy temple.*

PSALM 65:4

Surely, O LORD, you bless the righteous;
    you surround them with your favor as with
        a shield.

PSALM 5:12

Do not repay evil with evil or insult
with insult, but with blessing, because
to this you were called so that you
may inherit a blessing.

I PETER 3:9

He who has clean hands and a pure heart,
    who does not lift up his soul to an idol
    or swear by what is false.
He will receive blessing from the LORD
    and vindication from God his Savior.

PSALM 24:4–5

The Sovereign LORD declares, "I will make a
covenant of peace with them. . . . I will send down
showers in season; there will be showers of blessing.
The trees of the field will yield their fruit and the
ground will yield its crops; the people will be secure
in their land."

EZEKIEL 34:25–27

Blessed is the nation whose God is the LORD,
the people he chose for his inheritance.

PSALM 33:12

Looking at his disciples, [Jesus] said:
"Blessed are you who are poor,
for yours is the kingdom of God.
Blessed are you who hunger now,
for you will be satisfied.
Blessed are you who weep now,
for you will laugh.
Blessed are you when men hate you,
when they exclude you and insult you
and reject your name as evil,
because of the Son of Man.
Rejoice in that day and leap for joy, because great is
your reward in heaven."

LUKE 6:20–23

How great is your goodness,
which you have stored up for those who
fear you,
which you bestow in the sight of men
on those who take refuge in you.

PSALM 31:19

I am setting before you today a blessing ... the blessing if you obey the commands of the LORD your God that I am giving you today.

DEUTERONOMY 11:26–27

"I will satisfy the priests with abundance,
*   and my people will be filled with my bounty,"*
*   declares the LORD.*

JEREMIAH 31:14

"I will make you into a great nation
*   and I will bless you;*
I will make your name great,
*   and you will be a blessing.*
I will bless those who bless you,
*   and whoever curses you I will curse;*
and all peoples on earth
*   will be blessed through you," said the LORD.*

GENESIS 12:2–3

CELEBRATION

The LORD says,
"Be glad and rejoice forever
    in what I will create,
for I will create Jerusalem to be a
       delight
    and its people a joy.
I will rejoice over Jerusalem
    and take delight in my people."

ISAIAH 65:18–19

Praise God in his sanctuary;
*   praise him in his mighty heavens.*
Praise him for his acts of power;
*   praise him for his surpassing greatness.*
Praise him with the sounding of the trumpet,
*   praise him with the harp and lyre,*
praise him with tambourine and dancing,
*   praise him with the strings and flute,*
praise him with the clash of cymbals,
*   praise him with resounding cymbals.*
Let everything that has breath praise the LORD.

PSALM 150

The LORD declares,
"Maidens will dance and be glad,
young men and old as well.
I will turn their mourning into gladness;
I will give them comfort and joy instead
of sorrow."

JEREMIAH 31:13

I delight greatly in the LORD;
my soul rejoices in my God.
For he has clothed me with garments of salvation
and arrayed me in a robe of righteousness.

ISAIAH 61:10

Praise his name with dancing
and make music to him with tambourine
and harp.
For the LORD takes delight in his people;
he crowns the humble with salvation.
Let the saints rejoice in this honor
and sing for joy on their beds.

PSALM 149:3–5

CHALLENGES

Just as the sufferings of Christ flow over into our lives, so also through Christ our comfort overflows.

2 CORINTHIANS 1:5

Because the Sovereign LORD helps me,
*   I will not be disgraced.*
Therefore have I set my face like flint,
*   and I know I will not be put to shame.*

ISAIAH 50:7

[God] knows the way that I take; when he has tested me, I will come forth as gold.

JOB 23:10

Since we are surrounded by such a great cloud of witnesses, let us throw off everything that hinders and the sin that so easily entangles, and let us run with perseverance the race marked out for us. Let us fix our eyes on Jesus, the author and perfecter of our faith, who for the joy set before him endured the cross, scorning its shame, and sat down at the right hand of the throne of God. Consider him who endured such opposition from sinful men, so that you will not grow weary and lose heart.

HEBREWS 12:1–3

I consider that our present sufferings are not worth comparing with the glory that will be revealed in us.

ROMANS 8:18

For a little while you may have had to suffer grief in all kinds of trials. These have come so that your faith—of greater worth than gold, which perishes even though refined by fire—may be proved genuine and may result in praise, glory and honor when Jesus Christ is revealed.

1 PETER 1:6–7

[The LORD] has not despised or disdained
    the suffering of the afflicted one;
he has not hidden his face from him
    but has listened to his cry for help.

PSALM 22:24

For Christ's sake, I delight in weaknesses, in insults, in hardships, in persecutions, in difficulties. For when I am weak, then I am strong.

2 CORINTHIANS 12:10

CHANGE

We eagerly await a Savior from [heaven], the Lord Jesus Christ, who, by the power that enables him to bring everything under his control, will transform our lowly bodies so that they will be like his glorious body.

PHILIPPIANS 3:20–21

Jesus said, "I tell you the truth, unless you change and become like little children, you will never enter the kingdom of heaven."

MATTHEW 18:3

You were washed, you were sanctified, you were justified in the name of the Lord Jesus Christ and by the Spirit of our God.

I CORINTHIANS 6:11

Do not conform any longer to the pattern of this world, but be transformed by the renewing of your mind.

ROMANS 12:2

If anyone is in Christ, he is a new creation; the old has gone, the new has come!

2 CORINTHIANS 5:17

Praise be to the name of God for ever and ever;
    wisdom and power are his.
He changes times and seasons;
    he sets up kings and deposes them.
He gives wisdom to the wise
    and knowledge to the discerning.
He reveals deep and hidden things;
    he knows what lies in darkness,
    and light dwells with him.

DANIEL 2:20–22

This is what the sovereign LORD *says: "I will give them an undivided heart and put a new spirit in them; I will remove from them their heart of stone and give them a heart of flesh."*

EZEKIEL 11:19

"I the LORD do not change," says the LORD Almighty.

MALACHI 3:6

The Father of the heavenly lights . . . does not change like shifting shadows.

JAMES 1:17

Be made new in the attitude of your minds.

EPHESIANS 4:23

CHARACTER

Who is wise and understanding among you? Let him show it by his good life, by deeds done in the humility that comes from wisdom.

JAMES 3:13

The righteous will hold to their ways,
and those with clean hands will grow stronger.

JOB 17:9

The highway of the upright avoids evil;
he who guards his way guards his life.

PROVERBS 16:17

A man's ways are in full view of the LORD,
and he examines all his paths.

PROVERBS 5:21

We know that suffering produces perseverance; per-
severance, character; and character, hope. And hope
does not disappoint us, because God has poured out
his love into our hearts by the Holy Spirit, whom he
has given us.

ROMANS 5:3–5

Our conscience testifies that we have conducted ourselves in the world, and especially in our relations with you, in the holiness and sincerity that are from God. We have done so not according to worldly wisdom but according to God's grace.

2 CORINTHIANS 1:12

The noble man makes noble plans, and by noble deeds he stands.

ISAIAH 32:8

Set an example for the believers in speech, in life, in love, in faith and in purity.

1 TIMOTHY 4:12

Remind the people to be subject to rulers and authorities, to be obedient, to be ready to do whatever is good.

TITUS 3:1

The LORD is righteous, he loves justice; upright men will see his face.

PSALM 11:7

CHURCH

*Jesus said, "Blessed are you, Simon son of Jonah,
for this was not revealed to you by man, but by my
Father in heaven. And I tell you that you are Peter,
and on this rock I will build my church, and the
gates of Hades will not overcome it."*

MATTHEW 16:17–18

God's household . . . is the church
of the living God, the pillar and foundation of the truth.

I TIMOTHY 3:15

*[Christ] is the head of the body, the church; he is the
beginning and the firstborn from among the dead,
so that in everything he might have the supremacy.*

COLOSSIANS 1:18

*You are the body of Christ, and each one of you is a
part of it. And in the church God has appointed first
of all apostles, second prophets, third teachers, then
workers of miracles, also those having gifts of healing, those able to help others, those with gifts of
administration, and those speaking in different kinds
of tongues.*

I CORINTHIANS 12:27–28

You are no longer foreigners and aliens, but fellow citizens with God's people and members of God's household, built on the foundation of the apostles and prophets, with Christ Jesus himself as the chief cornerstone. In him the whole building is joined together and rises to become a holy temple in the Lord.

EPHESIANS 2:19–21

The body is a unit, though it is made up of many parts; and though all its parts are many, they form one body. So it is with Christ. For we were all baptized by one Spirit into one body—whether Jews or Greeks, slave or free—and we were all given the one Spirit to drink.

1 CORINTHIANS 12:12–13

Obey your leaders and submit to their authority. They keep watch over you as men who must give an account.

HEBREWS 13:17

Let us not give up meeting together, as some are in the habit of doing, but let us encourage one another—and all the more as you see the Day approaching.

HEBREWS 10:25

COMFORT

My comfort in my suffering is this:
  Your promise preserves my life.

PSALM 119:50

The LORD says,
"As a mother comforts her child,
    so will I comfort you;
    and you will be comforted over Jerusalem."

ISAIAH 66:13

The LORD is good,
  a refuge in times of trouble.
He cares for those who trust in him.

NAHUM 1:7

"I have seen his ways, but I will heal him;
    I will guide him and restore comfort to him,
    creating praise on the lips of the mourners
        in Israel.
Peace, peace, to those far and near,"
    says the LORD. "And I will heal them."

ISAIAH 57:18–19

The LORD is close to the brokenhearted
  and saves those who are crushed in spirit.

PSALM 34:18

Praise be to the God and Father of our Lord Jesus Christ, the Father of compassion and the God of all comfort, who comforts us in all our troubles, so that we can comfort those in any trouble with the comfort we ourselves have received from God.

2 CORINTHIANS 1:3–4

May your unfailing love be my comfort, according to your promise to your servant.

PSALM 119:76

Even though I walk
through the valley of the shadow
of death,
I will fear no evil,
for you are with me;
your rod and your staff,
they comfort me.

PSALM 23:4

Shout for joy, O heavens;
    rejoice, O earth;
    burst into song, O mountains!
For the LORD comforts his people
    and will have compassion on his afflicted ones.

ISAIAH 49:13

The Lamb at the center of the throne will be their
        shepherd;
    he will lead them to springs of living water.
And God will wipe away every tear from their eyes.

REVELATION 7:17

I remember your ancient laws, O LORD, and I find comfort in them.

PSALM 119:52

Give me a sign of your goodness,
    that my enemies may see it and be put to shame,
    for you, O LORD, have helped me and
        comforted me.

PSALM 86:17

[God] tends his flock like a shepherd:
  He gathers the lambs in his arms
and carries them close to his heart.

ISAIAH 40:11

Comfort, comfort my people,
  says your God.
Speak tenderly to Jerusalem,
  and proclaim to her
that her hard service has been completed,
  that her sin has been paid for,
that she has received from the LORD's hand
  double for all her sins.

ISAIAH 40:1–2

[Jesus'] disciples came to him, and he
began to teach them, saying: . . .
"Blessed are those who mourn,
  for they will be comforted."

MATTHEW 5:1–2, 4

COMMITMENT

Watch out that you do not lose what you have worked for, but that you may be rewarded fully. Anyone who runs ahead and does not continue in the teaching of Christ does not have God; whoever continues in the teaching has both the Father and the Son.

2 JOHN vv.8–9

The LORD said, "I will look on you with favor and make you fruitful and increase your numbers, and I will keep my covenant with you."

LEVITICUS 26:9

From everlasting to everlasting
*   the LORD's love is with those who fear him,*
*   and his righteousness with their children's*
*   children—*
with those who keep his covenant
*   and remember to obey his precepts.*

PSALM 103:17–18

Be joyful always; pray continually; give thanks in all circumstances, for this is God's will for you in Christ Jesus.

1 THESSALONIANS 5:16–18

Commit your way to the LORD;
  trust in him and he will do this:
He will make your righteousness shine like the dawn,
  the justice of your cause like the noonday sun.

PSALM 37:5–6

Commit to the LORD whatever you do, and your plans will succeed.

PROVERBS 16:3

"I will give them singleness of heart and action, so that they will always fear me for their own good and the good of their children after them. I will make an everlasting covenant with them: I will never stop doing good to them, and I will inspire them to fear me, so that they will never turn away from me," declares the LORD.

JEREMIAH 32:39–40

I will establish my covenant as an everlasting covenant between me and you and your descendants after you for the generations to come, to be your God and the God of your descendants after you.

GENESIS 17:7

Jesus said, "I am coming soon. Hold on to what you have, so that no one will take your crown. Him who overcomes I will make a pillar in the temple of my God. Never again will he leave it. I will write on him the name of my God and the name of the city of my God, the new Jerusalem, which is coming down out of heaven from my God; and I will also write on him my new name."

REVELATION 3:11–12

He is the LORD our God;
   his judgments are in all the earth.
He remembers his covenant forever,
   the word he commanded, for a
      thousand generations,
the covenant he made with Abraham,
   the oath he swore to Isaac.

PSALM 105:7–9

I know whom I have believed, and am convinced that he is able to guard what I have entrusted to him for that day.

2 TIMOTHY 1:12

"If your sons keep my covenant
and the statutes I teach them,
then their sons will sit
on your throne for ever and ever,"
says the LORD.

PSALM 132:12

*Test everything. Hold on to the good. Avoid every
kind of evil. May God himself, the God of peace,
sanctify you through and through. May your whole
spirit, soul and body be kept blameless at the coming of our Lord Jesus Christ. The one who calls you
is faithful and he will do it.*

1 THESSALONIANS 5:21–24

*The eyes of the LORD range throughout the earth to
strengthen those whose hearts are fully committed
to him.*

2 CHRONICLES 16:9

*Those who suffer according to God's will should
commit themselves to their faithful Creator and continue to do good.*

1 PETER 4:19

COMMUNICATION

From the fruit of his lips a man
enjoys good things.

PROVERBS 13:2

*From the fruit of his mouth a man's stomach
is filled;
with the harvest from his lips he is satisfied.*

PROVERBS 18:20

May the words of my mouth and the
meditation of my heart
be pleasing in your sight,
O LORD, my Rock and my
Redeemer.

PSALM 19:14

*Always be prepared to give an answer to everyone
who asks you to give the reason for the hope that
you have. But do this with gentleness and respect.*

1 PETER 3:15

*If anyone speaks, he should do it as one speaking
the very words of God.*

1 PETER 4:11

Confess your sins to each other and pray for each other so that you may be healed.

JAMES 5:16

He who guards his lips guards his life.

PROVERBS 13:3

We will no longer be infants, tossed back and forth by the waves, and blown here and there by every wind of teaching and by the cunning and craftiness of men in their deceitful scheming. Instead, speaking the truth in love, we will in all things grow up into him who is the Head, that is, Christ.

EPHESIANS 4:14–15

The mouth of the righteous man utters wisdom,
*   and his tongue speaks what is just.*
The law of his God is in his heart;
*   his feet do not slip.*

PSALM 37:30–31

He who holds his tongue is wise. The tongue of the righteous is choice silver.

PROVERBS 10:19–20

The tongue that brings healing is a
tree of life.

PROVERBS 15:4

Let your conversation be always full of grace,
seasoned with salt, so that you may know how to
answer everyone.

COLOSSIANS 4:6

The Sovereign LORD has given me an instructed
tongue,
to know the word that sustains the weary.

ISAIAH 50:4

Set a guard over my mouth,
O LORD;
keep watch over the door of
my lips.

PSALM 141:3

If anyone is never at fault in what he says, he is a
perfect man, able to keep his whole body in check.

JAMES 3:2

A word aptly spoken
    is like apples of gold in settings
        of silver.

PROVERBS 25:11

A wise man's heart guides his mouth,
    and his lips promote instruction.
Pleasant words are a honeycomb,
    sweet to the soul and healing to the bones.

PROVERBS 16:23–24

A man finds joy in giving an apt
    reply—
and how good is a timely word!

PROVERBS 15:23

A gentle answer turns away wrath,
    but a harsh word stirs up anger.
The tongue of the wise commends knowledge.

PROVERBS 15:1–2

COMPASSION

Be kind and compassionate to one another, forgiving each other, just as in Christ God forgave you. Be imitators of God, therefore, as dearly loved children and live a life of love, just as Christ loved us and gave himself up for us as a fragrant offering and sacrifice to God

EPHESIANS 4:32–5:2

Let your compassion come to me that I may live, for your law is my delight.

PSALM 119:77

The LORD is gracious and righteous;
*   our God is full of compassion.*
The LORD protects the simplehearted;
*   when I was in great need, he saved me.*

PSALM 116:5–6

The LORD longs to be gracious to you;
*   he rises to show you compassion.*
For the LORD is a God of justice.
*   Blessed are all who wait for him!*

ISAIAH 30:18

You, O LORD, are a compassionate
and gracious God,
slow to anger, abounding in love
and faithfulness.

PSALM 86:15

The LORD is good to all;
he has compassion on all he has made.

PSALM 145:9

"Though the mountains be shaken
and the hills be removed,
yet my unfailing love for you will not be shaken
nor my covenant of peace be removed,"
says the LORD, who has compassion on you.

ISAIAH 54:10

"I will betroth you to me forever;
I will betroth you in righteousness
and justice,
in love and compassion,"
declares the LORD.

HOSEA 2:19

Your compassion is great, O LORD;
preserve my life according to
your laws.

PSALM 119:156

As a father has compassion on his children,
so the LORD has compassion on those who
fear him.

PSALM 103:13

Because of the LORD's great love we are not
consumed,
for his compassions never fail.
They are new every morning;
great is your faithfulness.

LAMENTATIONS 3:22–23

The LORD your God is gracious and
compassionate. He will not turn his
face from you if you return to him.

2 CHRONICLES 30:9

Even in darkness light dawns for the upright,
for the gracious and compassionate and
righteous man.

PSALM 112:4

You will again have compassion on us;
you will tread our sins underfoot
and hurl all our iniquities into the depths of
the sea.

MICAH 7:19

Live in harmony with one another;
be sympathetic, love as brothers, be
compassionate and humble ... so
that you may inherit a blessing.

I PETER 3:8–9

The LORD is gracious and compassionate.
He provides food for those who fear him;
he remembers his covenant forever.

PSALM 111:4–5

They will neither hunger nor thirst,
nor will the desert heat or the sun beat
upon them.
He who has compassion on them will guide them
and lead them beside springs of water.

ISAIAH 49:10

CONFIDENCE

The LORD will be your confidence
and will keep your foot from
being snared.

PROVERBS 3:26

*The effect of righteousness will be quietness and
confidence forever.*

ISAIAH 32:17

*This is the confidence we have in approaching God:
that if we ask anything according to his will, he
hears us. And if we know that he hears us—whatever we ask—we know that we have what we asked
of him.*

1 JOHN 5:14–15

*Let us then approach the throne of grace with confi-
dence, so that we may receive mercy and find grace
to help us in our time of need.*

HEBREWS 4:16

*The LORD himself goes before you and will be with
you; he will never leave you nor forsake you. Do
not be afraid; do not be discouraged.*

DEUTERONOMY 31:8

Such confidence as this is ours through Christ before God. Not that we are competent in ourselves to claim anything for ourselves, but our competence comes from God. He has made us competent.

2 CORINTHIANS 3:4–6

Blessed is the man who trusts in
the LORD,
whose confidence is in him.

JEREMIAH 17:7

The LORD is the stronghold of my life—
of whom shall I be afraid? . . .
Though an army besiege me,
my heart will not fear;
though war break out against me,
even then will I be confident.

PSALM 27:1, 3

Do not throw away your confidence;
it will be richly rewarded.

HEBREWS 10:35

[God] who began a good work in you will carry it on to completion until the day of Christ Jesus.

PHILIPPIANS 1:6

We say with confidence, "The LORD is my helper; I will not be afraid. What can man do to me?"

HEBREWS 13:6

I eagerly expect and hope that I will in no way be ashamed, but will have sufficient courage so that now as always Christ will be exalted in my body, whether by life or by death.

PHILIPPIANS 1:20

When I called, [O LORD] you
    answered me;
  you made me bold and
    stouthearted.

PSALM 138:3

We have come to share in Christ if we hold firmly till the end the confidence we had at first.

HEBREWS 3:14

I can do everything through [Christ] who gives me strength.

PHILIPPIANS 4:13

[The Lord] said to me, "My grace is sufficient for you, for my power is made perfect in weakness." Therefore I will boast all the more gladly about my weaknesses, so that Christ's power may rest on me.

2 CORINTHIANS 12:9

When I am afraid,
    I will trust in you.
In God, whose word I praise,
    in God I trust; I will not be afraid.
    What can mortal man do to me?

PSALM 56:3–4

If our hearts do not condemn us, we have confidence before God and receive from him anything we ask, because we obey his commands and do what pleases him. And this is his command: to believe in the name of his Son, Jesus Christ, and to love one another as he commanded us.

1 JOHN 3:21–23

CONFLICT

He ransoms me unharmed
from the battle waged against me,
even though many oppose me.

PSALM 55:18

Do not be quickly provoked in your spirit.

ECCLESIASTES 7:9

It is to a man's honor to avoid strife.

PROVERBS 20:3

*Agree with one another so that there may be no
divisions among you.*

1 CORINTHIANS 1:10

*Jesus said, "I pray also for those who will believe in
me. . . . May they be brought to complete unity to let
the world know that you sent me."*

JOHN 17:20, 23

A fool shows his annoyance at once,
but a prudent man overlooks
an insult.

PROVERBS 12:16

There should be no division in the body, but ...
its parts should have equal concern for each other.
If one part suffers, every part suffers with it; if one
part is honored, every part rejoices with it.

1 CORINTHIANS 12:25–26

Hatred stirs up dissension, but love covers over all wrongs.

PROVERBS 10:12

Do everything without complaining or arguing, so
that you may become blameless and pure, children
of God without fault in a crooked and depraved
generation, in which you shine like stars in the uni-
verse as you hold out the word of life.

PHILIPPIANS 2:14–16

Make every effort to keep the unity of the Spirit.

EPHESIANS 4:3

CONTENTMENT

Keep your lives free from the love of money and be content with what you have, because God has said, "Never will I leave you; never will I forsake you."

HEBREWS 13:5

Better a little with righteousness than much gain with injustice.

PROVERBS 16:8

Godliness with contentment is great gain.

I TIMOTHY 6:6

The fear of the LORD leads to life: Then one rests content, untouched by trouble.

PROVERBS 19:23

I have learned to be content whatever the circumstances. I know what it is to be in need, and I know what it is to have plenty. I have learned the secret of being content in any and every situation, whether well fed or hungry, whether living in plenty or in want.

PHILIPPIANS 4:11–12

Each one should retain the place in life that the Lord assigned to him and to which God has called him.

1 CORINTHIANS 7:17

If we have food and clothing, we will be content with that.

1 TIMOTHY 6:8

*Better the little that the righteous have
    than the wealth of many wicked;
for the power of the wicked will be broken,
    but the LORD upholds the righteous.*

PSALM 37:16–17

Better one handful with tranquility
    than two handfuls with toil
    and chasing after the wind.

ECCLESIASTES 4:6

COURAGE

The LORD is my light and my salvation—
*   whom shall I fear?*
The LORD is the stronghold of my life—
*   of whom shall I be afraid?*

PSALM 27:1

I can do everything through [Christ] who gives me strength.

PHILIPPIANS 4:13

The LORD said, "Be strong and very courageous. Be careful to obey all the law my servant Moses gave you; do not turn from it to the right or to the left, that you may be successful wherever you go."

JOSHUA 1:7

To live is Christ and to die is gain.

PHILIPPIANS 1:21

Hezekiah said, "Be strong and courageous. Do not be afraid or discouraged because of the king of Assyria and the vast army with him, for there is a greater power with us than with him. With him is only the arm of flesh, but with us is the LORD our God to help us and to fight our battles."

2 CHRONICLES 32:7–8

Be on your guard; stand firm in the faith; be men of courage; be strong.

1 CORINTHIANS 16:13

Moses said, "Be strong and courageous. Do not be afraid or terrified ... for the LORD your God goes with you; he will never leave you nor forsake you."

DEUTERONOMY 31:6

The LORD said, "Have I not commanded you? Be strong and courageous. Do not be terrified; do not be discouraged, for the LORD your God will be with you wherever you go."

JOSHUA 1:9

This is what the LORD says to you: "Do not be afraid or discouraged.... For the battle is not yours, but God's."

2 CHRONICLES 20:15

Jesus immediately said to them: "Take courage! It is I. Don't be afraid."

MATTHEW 14:27

Be strong and take heart,
   all you who hope in the LORD.

PSALM 31:24

Act with courage, and may the LORD be with those who do well.

2 CHRONICLES 19:11

I am the LORD, your God,
   who takes hold of your right hand
and says to you, Do not fear;
   I will help you.

ISAIAH 41:13

Christ is faithful as a son over God's house. And we are his house, if we hold on to our courage and the hope of which we boast.

HEBREWS 3:6

Be strong and courageous. Do not
be afraid or discouraged.

1 CHRONICLES 22:13

Strengthen the feeble hands,
    steady the knees that give way;
say to those with fearful hearts,
   "Be strong, do not fear;
your God will come,
    he will come with vengeance;
with divine retribution
    he will come to save you."

ISAIAH 35:3–4

When you pass through the waters,
    I will be with you;
and when you pass through the rivers,
    they will not sweep over you.
When you walk through the fire,
    you will not be burned;
    the flames will not set you ablaze.
For I am the LORD, *your God,*
    the Holy One of Israel, your Savior. . . .
You are precious and honored in my sight.

ISAIAH 43:2–4

DAILY WALK

Since we live by the Spirit, let us keep in step with the Spirit.

GALATIANS 5:25

This is what the LORD says:
"Stand at the crossroads and look;
*   ask for the ancient paths,*
ask where the good way is, and walk in it,
*   and you will find rest for your souls."*

JEREMIAH 6:16

Just as you received Christ Jesus as Lord, continue to
live in him, rooted and built up in him, strengthened
in the faith as you were taught, and overflowing
with thankfulness.

COLOSSIANS 2:6–7

God did not call us to be impure, but to live a holy life.

I THESSALONIANS 4:7

Walk in all the way that the LORD your God has
commanded you, so that you may live and prosper
and prolong your days in the land that you will
possess.

DEUTERONOMY 5:33

We pray this in order that you may live a life worthy of the Lord and may please him in every way: bearing fruit in every good work, growing in the knowledge of God.

COLOSSIANS 1:10

Be very careful, then, how you live— not as unwise but as wise.

EPHESIANS 5:15

*He who walks righteously
    and speaks what is right,
who rejects gain from extortion
    and keeps his hand from accepting bribes,
who stops his ears against plots of murder
    and shuts his eyes against contemplating evil—
this is the man who will dwell on the heights,
    whose refuge will be the mountain fortress.
His bread will be supplied,
    and water will not fail him.*

ISAIAH 33:15–16

DECISIONS

If any of you lacks wisdom, he should ask God,
who gives generously to all without finding fault,
and it will be given to him.

JAMES 1:5

Preserve sound judgment and discernment,
    do not let them out of your sight;
they will be life for you,
    an ornament to grace your neck.
Then you will go on your way in safety,
    and your foot will not stumble.

PROVERBS 3:21–23

I have set before you life and death, blessings and
curses. Now choose life, so that you and your chil-
dren may live.

DEUTERONOMY 30:19

Commit your way to the LORD;
    trust in him and he will do this:
He will make your righteousness
        shine like the dawn,
    the justice of your cause like the
        noonday sun.

PSALM 37:5–6

This is what the LORD Almighty says: "Give careful thought to your ways."

HAGGAI 1:5

The heart of the discerning acquires knowledge;
the ears of the wise seek it out.

PROVERBS 18:15

Who has known the mind of the Lord that he may instruct him? But we have the mind of Christ.

1 CORINTHIANS 2:16

Trust in the LORD with all your heart
and lean not on your own understanding;
in all your ways acknowledge him,
and he will make your paths straight.

PROVERBS 3:5–6

Jesus said, "I will ask the Father, and he will give you another Counselor to be with you forever— the Spirit of truth."

JOHN 14:16

DELIVERANCE

The righteous cry out, and the LORD hears them;
he delivers them from all their troubles.

PSALM 34:17

The Lord knows how to rescue godly men from trials.

2 PETER 2:9

They cried out to the LORD in their trouble,
and he delivered them from their distress.

PSALM 107:6

"Because he loves me," says the LORD,
"I will rescue him;
I will protect him, for he acknowledges
my name.
He will call upon me, and I will answer him;
I will be with him in trouble,
I will deliver him and honor him."

PSALM 91:14–15

The LORD is my rock, my fortress and my deliverer.

2 SAMUEL 22:2

The angel of the LORD encamps
      around those who fear him,
and he delivers them.

PSALM 34:7

For you, O LORD, have delivered my soul
      from death,
my eyes from tears,
my feet from stumbling.

PSALM 116:8

You are my hiding place;
    you will protect me from trouble
    and surround me with songs of
        deliverance.

PSALM 32:7

He will deliver the needy who cry out,
    the afflicted who have no one to help.
He will take pity on the weak and the needy
    and save the needy from death.

PSALM 72:12–13

DETERMINATION

Stand firm. Let nothing move you. Always give yourselves fully to the work of the Lord, because you know that your labor in the Lord is not in vain.

1 CORINTHIANS 15:58

Be on your guard; stand firm in the faith; be men of courage; be strong.

1 CORINTHIANS 16:13

We are hard pressed on every side, but not crushed; perplexed, but not in despair; persecuted, but not abandoned; struck down, but not destroyed.

2 CORINTHIANS 4:8–9

Jesus said, "I am coming soon. Hold on to what you have, so that no one will take your crown."

REVELATION 3:11

Because the Sovereign LORD helps me,
    I will not be disgraced.
Therefore have I set my face like flint,
    and I know I will not be put to shame.

ISAIAH 50:7

Let us not become weary in doing good, for at the proper time we will reap a harvest if we do not give up.

GALATIANS 6:9

[God] alone is my rock and my salvation;
he is my fortress, I will not be shaken.

PSALM 62:6

When the storm has swept by, the wicked are gone,
but the righteous stand firm forever.

PROVERBS 10:25

As for you, be strong and do not give up, for your work will be rewarded.

2 CHRONICLES 15:7

Your enemy the devil prowls around like a roaring
lion looking for someone to devour. Resist him,
standing firm in the faith, because you know that
your brothers throughout the world are undergoing
the same kind of sufferings.

1 PETER 5:8–9

DISCIPLESHIP

Jesus said, "If you hold to my teaching, you are really my disciples. Then you will know the truth, and the truth will set you free."

JOHN 8:31–32

In the presence of God and of Christ Jesus, who will judge the living and the dead, and in view of his appearing and his kingdom, I give you this charge: Preach the Word; be prepared in season and out of season; correct, rebuke and encourage—with great patience and careful instruction.

2 TIMOTHY 4:1–2

Jesus said to his disciples, "If anyone would come after me, he must deny himself and take up his cross and follow me. For whoever wants to save his life will lose it, but whoever loses his life for me will find it."

MATTHEW 16:24–25

Jesus said, "A new command I give you: Love one another. As I have loved you, so you must love one another. By this all men will know that you are my disciples, if you love one another."

JOHN 13:34–35

Jesus said, "My sheep listen to my voice; I know them, and they follow me."

JOHN 10:27

Jesus said, "Whoever serves me must follow me; and where I am, my servant also will be. My Father will honor the one who serves me."

JOHN 12:26

If they obey and serve him,
they will spend the rest of their
days in prosperity
and their years in contentment.

JOB 36:11

Jesus said, "I am the light of the world. Whoever follows me will never walk in darkness, but will have the light of life."

JOHN 8:12

Jesus said, "This is to my Father's glory, that you bear much fruit, showing yourselves to be my disciples."

JOHN 15:8

DOUBT

[Abraham] did not waver through unbelief regarding the promise of God, but was strengthened in his faith and gave glory to God, being fully persuaded that God had power to do what he had promised.

ROMANS 4:20–21

Jesus said, "Surely I am with you always, to the very end of the age."

MATTHEW 28:20

Jesus said, "I tell you the truth, if anyone says to this mountain, 'Go, throw yourself into the sea,' and does not doubt in his heart but believes that what he says will happen, it will be done for him."

MARK 11:23

What if some did not have faith? Will their lack of faith nullify God's faithfulness? Not at all!

ROMANS 3:3–4

Jesus said, "Don't be afraid; just believe."

MARK 5:36

Be merciful to those who doubt.

JUDE v.22

Jesus said, "Are not five sparrows sold for two pennies? Yet not one of them is forgotten by God. Indeed, the very hairs of your head are all numbered. Don't be afraid; you are worth more than many sparrows."

LUKE 12:6–7

Let us hold unswervingly to the hope we profess, for he who promised is faithful.

HEBREWS 10:23

Jesus said, "Everything is possible for him who believes." Immediately the boy's father exclaimed, "I do believe; help me overcome my unbelief!"

MARK 9:23–24

The apostles said to the Lord, "Increase our faith!" He replied, "If you have faith as small as a mustard seed, you can say to this mulberry tree, 'Be uprooted and planted in the sea,' and it will obey you."

LUKE 17:5–6

ENCOURAGEMENT

You hear, O LORD, the desire of the afflicted;
*   you encourage them, and you listen to their cry.*

PSALM 10:17

Encourage one another and build each other up, just
as in fact you are doing. . . . We urge you, brothers,
. . . encourage the timid, help the weak, be patient
with everyone.

1 THESSALONIANS 5:11, 14

May our Lord Jesus Christ himself and God our
Father, who loved us and by his grace gave us
eternal encouragement and good hope, encourage
your hearts and strengthen you in every good deed
and word.

2 THESSALONIANS 2:16–17

Everything that was written in the past was written
to teach us, so that through endurance and the
encouragement of the Scriptures we might have hope.

ROMANS 15:4

Let us not give up meeting together, as some are in
the habit of doing, but let us encourage one another—
and all the more as you see the Day approaching.

HEBREWS 10:25

Why are you downcast, O my soul?
Why so disturbed within me?
Put your hope in God,
for I will yet praise him,
my Savior and my God.
My soul is downcast within me;
therefore I will remember you.

PSALM 42:5–6

To you, O LORD, I lift up my soul;
in you I trust, O my God.
Do not let me be put to shame,
nor let my enemies triumph over me.
No one whose hope is in you
will ever be put to shame.

PSALM 25:1–3

Do not be fainthearted or afraid; do not be
terrified. . . . For the LORD your God is the one
who goes with you to fight for you against your
enemies to give you victory.

DEUTERONOMY 20:3–4

ETERNAL LIFE

Jesus said, "This is eternal life: that they may know you, the only true God, and Jesus Christ, whom you have sent."

JOHN 17:3

Jesus said, "I tell you the truth, whoever hears my word and believes him who sent me has eternal life and will not be condemned; he has crossed over from death to life."

JOHN 5:24

Having been justified by his grace, we might become heirs having the hope of eternal life.

TITUS 3:7

This is the testimony: God has given us eternal life, and this life is in his Son. He who has the Son has life; he who does not have the Son of God does not have life.

1 JOHN 5:11–12

Jesus said to her, "I am the resurrection and the life. He who believes in me will live, even though he dies; and whoever lives and believes in me will never die."

JOHN 11:25–26

Now that you have been set free from sin and have become slaves to God, the benefit you reap leads to holiness, and the result is eternal life. For the wages of sin is death, but the gift of God is eternal life in Christ Jesus our Lord.

ROMANS 6:22–23

Jesus said, "For God so loved the world that he gave his one and only Son, that whoever believes in him shall not perish but have eternal life."

JOHN 3:16

Jesus said to them, "I tell you the truth, unless you eat the flesh of the Son of Man and drink his blood, you have no life in you. Whoever eats my flesh and drinks my blood has eternal life, and I will raise him up at the last day."

JOHN 6:53–54

Jesus said, "My sheep listen to my voice; I know them, and they follow me. I give them eternal life, and they shall never perish; no one can snatch them out of my hand."

JOHN 10:27–28

EVANGELISM

Jesus said, "Peace be with you! As the Father has sent me, I am sending you."

JOHN 20:21

Jesus said, "You are the light of the world. A city on a hill cannot be hidden. Neither do people light a lamp and put it under a bowl. Instead they put it on its stand, and it gives light to everyone in the house. In the same way, let your light shine before men, that they may see your good deeds and praise your Father in heaven."

MATTHEW 5:14–16

I pray that you may be active in sharing your faith, so that you will have a full understanding of every good thing we have in Christ.

PHILEMON v.6

Jesus said, "Whoever acknowledges me before men, I will also acknowledge him before my Father in heaven."

MATTHEW 10:32

Jesus said, "No one lights a lamp and hides it in a jar or puts it under a bed. Instead, he puts it on a stand, so that those who come in can see the light."

 LUKE 8:16

Jesus said, "All authority in heaven and on earth has been given to me. Therefore go and make disciples of all nations, baptizing them in the name of the Father and of the Son and of the Holy Spirit, and teaching them to obey everything I have commanded you. And surely I am with you always, to the very end of the age."

MATTHEW 28:18–20

Jesus said, "You will be my witnesses in Jerusalem, and in all Judea and Samaria, and to the ends of the earth."

ACTS 1:8

Jesus said, "This gospel of the kingdom will be preached in the whole world as a testimony to all nations, and then the end will come."

MATTHEW 24:14

I am not ashamed of the gospel, because it is the power of God for the salvation of everyone who believes.

ROMANS 1:16

In your hearts set apart Christ as Lord. Always be prepared to give an answer to everyone who asks you to give the reason for the hope that you have. But do this with gentleness and respect.

1 PETER 3:15

Jesus said, "I tell you, whoever acknowledges me before men, the Son of Man will also acknowledge him before the angels of God."

LUKE 12:8

Even when I am old and gray,
*   do not forsake me, O God,*
till I declare your power to the next generation,
*   your might to all who are to come.*

PSALM 71:18

Give thanks to the LORD, call on his name;
*   make known among the nations what he*
*   has done.*
Sing to him, sing praise to him;
*   tell of all his wonderful acts.*

1 CHRONICLES 16:8–9

How beautiful on the mountains
*   are the feet of those who bring good news,*
who proclaim peace,
*   who bring good tidings,*
*   who proclaim salvation,*
who say to Zion,
*   "Your God reigns!"*

ISAIAH 52:7

Those who are wise will shine like the brightness of
the heavens, and those who lead many to righteous-
ness, like the stars for ever and ever.

DANIEL 12:3

Jesus said, "Go into all the world and preach the good news to all creation."

MARK 16:15

Do everything without complaining or arguing, so
that you may become blameless and pure, children
of God without fault in a crooked and depraved
generation, in which you shine like stars in the uni-
verse as you hold out the word of life.

PHILIPPIANS 2:14–16

EXPECTATIONS

I wait for the LORD, my soul waits,
   and in his word I put my hope.

PSALM 130:5

*I eagerly expect and hope that I will in no way be
ashamed, but will have sufficient courage so that
now as always Christ will be exalted in my body,
whether by life or by death.*

PHILIPPIANS 1:20

Wait for the LORD;
   be strong and take heart
   and wait for the LORD.

PSALM 27:14

*You do not lack any spiritual gift as you eagerly
wait for our Lord Jesus Christ to be revealed. He
will keep you strong to the end, so that you will be
blameless on the day of our Lord Jesus Christ.*

1 CORINTHIANS 1:7–8

The LORD says,
"Those who hope in me will not
be disappointed."

ISAIAH 49:23

As surely as the sun rises,
[the LORD] will appear;
he will come to us like the winter rains,
like the spring rains that water the earth.

HOSEA 6:3

In the morning, O LORD, you hear my voice;
in the morning I lay my requests before you
and wait in expectation.

PSALM 5:3

In you, [O LORD], our fathers put their trust;
they trusted and you delivered them.
They cried to you and were saved;
in you they trusted and were not disappointed.

PSALM 22:4–5

FAITH

Build yourselves up in your most holy faith and pray in the Holy Spirit. Keep yourselves in God's love as you wait for the mercy of our Lord Jesus Christ to bring you to eternal life.

JUDE vv.20–21

Faith is being sure of what we hope for and certain of what we do not see.

HEBREWS 11:1

Through [Christ] you believe in God, who raised him from the dead and glorified him, and so your faith and hope are in God.

1 PETER 1:21

It is by grace you have been saved, through faith— and this not from yourselves, it is the gift of God— not by works, so that no one can boast.

EPHESIANS 2:8–9

Jesus said, "I tell you the truth, anyone who has faith in me will do what I have been doing. He will do even greater things than these, because I am going to the Father."

JOHN 14:12

Jesus said, "I tell you the truth, if you have faith as small as a mustard seed, you can say to this mountain, 'Move from here to there' and it will move. Nothing will be impossible for you."

MATTHEW 17:20

[Abraham] did not waver through unbelief regarding the promise of God, but was strengthened in his faith and gave glory to God, being fully persuaded that God had power to do what he had promised.

ROMANS 4:20–21

In the gospel a righteousness from God is revealed, a righteousness that is by faith from first to last, just as it is written: "The righteous will live by faith."

ROMANS 1:17

Since we have been justified through faith, we have peace with God through our Lord Jesus Christ, through whom we have gained access by faith into this grace in which we now stand. And we rejoice in the hope of the glory of God.

ROMANS 5:1–2

FAITHFULNESS

[God] guards the course of the just
  and protects the way of his faithful ones.

PROVERBS 2:8

To the faithful, [O LORD,] you
    show yourself faithful,
to the blameless you show
    yourself blameless.

2 SAMUEL 22:26

My eyes will be on the faithful in the land,
  that they may dwell with me;
he whose walk is blameless
  will minister to me.

PSALM 101:6

The fruit of the Spirit is love, joy, peace, patience,
kindness, goodness, faithfulness, gentleness and self-
control. Against such things there is no law.

GALATIANS 5:22–23

Those who plan what is good
    find love and faithfulness.

PROVERBS 14:22

Jesus said, "These are the words of him who is the First and the Last, who died and came to life again: I know your afflictions and your poverty—yet you are rich!... Be faithful, even to the point of death, and I will give you the crown of life."

REVELATION 2:8–10

The LORD loves the just
  and will not forsake his faithful ones.

PSALM 37:28

Love the LORD, all his saints!
The LORD preserves the faithful,
but the proud he pays back in full.

PSALM 31:23

Let love and faithfulness never leave you;
  bind them around your neck,
  write them on the tablet of your heart.
Then you will win favor and a good name
  in the sight of God and man.

PROVERBS 3:3–4

FAMILY

God sets the lonely in families.

PSALM 68:6

How great is the love the Father has lavished on us, that we should be called children of God! And that is what we are!

1 JOHN 3:1

You did not receive a spirit that makes you a slave again to fear, but you received the Spirit of sonship. And by him we cry, "Abba, Father." The Spirit himself testifies with our spirit that we are God's children.

ROMANS 8:15–16

Sons are a heritage from the LORD,
children a reward from him....
Blessed is the man
whose quiver is full of them.

PSALM 127:3, 5

*Train a child in the way he should go,
    and when he is old he will not turn from it.*

PROVERBS 22:6

If you belong to Christ, then you are Abraham's seed, and heirs according to the promise.

GALATIANS 3:29

Whoever loves his brother lives in the light, and there is nothing in him to make him stumble.

1 JOHN 2:10

Both the one who makes men holy and those who are made holy are of the same family. So Jesus is not ashamed to call them brothers.

HEBREWS 2:11

Children's children are a crown to the aged,
*   and parents are the pride of their children.*

PROVERBS 17:6

The LORD God said, "It is not good for the man to be alone. I will make a helper suitable for him."
... For this reason a man will leave his father and mother and be united to his wife, and they will become one flesh.

GENESIS 2:18, 24

FEAR

There is no fear in love. But perfect love drives out fear.

1 JOHN 4:18

The LORD is my light and my salvation—
    whom shall I fear?
The LORD is the stronghold of my life—
    of whom shall I be afraid?

PSALM 27:1

Do not be afraid. Stand firm and you will see the deliverance the LORD will bring you today.

EXODUS 14:13

I sought the LORD, and he answered me;
    he delivered me from all my fears.

PSALM 34:4

Do not fear, for I am with you;
    do not be dismayed, for I am your God.
I will strengthen you and help you;
    I will uphold you with my righteous right hand.

ISAIAH 41:10

The LORD has taken away your punishment,
he has turned back your enemy.
The LORD, the King of Israel, is with you;
never again will you fear any harm.

ZEPHANIAH 3:15

Jesus said, "Do not be afraid, little flock, for your Father has been pleased to give you the kingdom."

LUKE 12:32

Even though I walk
through the valley of the shadow of death,
I will fear no evil,
for you are with me;
your rod and your staff,
they comfort me.

PSALM 23:4

When I am afraid,
I will trust in you, [O God].

PSALM 56:3

FELLOWSHIP

Let us therefore make every effort to do what leads to peace and to mutual edification.

ROMANS 14:19

If we walk in the light, as [God] is in the light, we have fellowship with one another.

I JOHN 1:7

Live in harmony with one another; be sympathetic, love as brothers, be compassionate and humble. Do not repay evil with evil or insult with insult, but with blessing, because to this you were called so that you may inherit a blessing.

I PETER 3:8–9

Our fellowship is with the Father and with his Son, Jesus Christ.

I JOHN 1:3

In humility consider others better than yourselves. Each of you should look not only to your own interests, but also to the interests of others.

PHILIPPIANS 2:3–4

Let the word of Christ dwell in you richly as you teach and admonish one another with all wisdom, and as you sing psalms, hymns and spiritual songs with gratitude in your hearts to God.

COLOSSIANS 3:16

Jesus said, "Where two or three come together in my name, there am I with them."

MATTHEW 18:20

*How good and pleasant it is
    when brothers live together in unity!
It is like precious oil poured on the head,
    running down on the beard,
running down on Aaron's beard,
    down upon the collar of his robes.
It is as if the dew of Hermon
    were falling on Mount Zion.
For there the LORD bestows his blessing,
    even life forevermore.*

PSALM 133

FINANCES

Let no debt remain outstanding, except the continuing debt to love one another, for he who loves his fellowman has fulfilled the law.

ROMANS 13:8

"Bring the whole tithe into the storehouse, that there may be food in my house. Test me in this," says the LORD Almighty, "and see if I will not throw open the floodgates of heaven and pour out so much blessing that you will not have room enough for it."

MALACHI 3:10

Whoever trusts in his riches will fall,
    but the righteous will thrive like a green leaf.

PROVERBS 11:28

Jesus said, "Go, sell everything you have and give to the poor, and you will have treasure in heaven."

MARK 10:21

A good man leaves an inheritance for his
        children's children,
    but a sinner's wealth is stored up for the
        righteous.

PROVERBS 13:22

*Keep your lives free from the love of money and be
content with what you have, because God has said,
"Never will I leave you; never will I forsake you."*

HEBREWS 13:5

He who gathers money little by little makes it grow.

PROVERBS 13:11

*Remember the LORD your God, for it is he who
gives you the ability to produce wealth, and so
confirms his covenant, which he swore to your
forefathers, as it is today.*

DEUTERONOMY 8:18

*My God will meet all your needs according to his
glorious riches in Christ Jesus.*

PHILIPPIANS 4:19

*Honor the LORD with your wealth,
    with the firstfruits of all your crops;
then your barns will be filled to overflowing,
    and your vats will brim over with new wine.*

PROVERBS 3:9–10

FORGIVENESS

Blessed is he
   whose transgressions are forgiven,
   whose sins are covered.
Blessed is the man
   whose sin the LORD does not count against him.

PSALM 32:1–2

If we confess our sins, [God] is faithful and just and will forgive us our sins and purify us from all unrighteousness.

I JOHN 1:9

When you were dead in your sins and in the uncircumcision of your sinful nature, God made you alive with Christ. He forgave us all our sins, having canceled the written code, with its regulations, that was against us and that stood opposed to us; he took it away, nailing it to the cross.

COLOSSIANS 2:13–14

As far as the east is from the west, so far has he removed our transgressions from us.

PSALM 103:12

Jesus said, "When you stand praying, if you hold anything against anyone, forgive him, so that your Father in heaven may forgive you your sins."

MARK 11:25

The Lord our God is merciful and forgiving.

DANIEL 9:9

Jesus said, "If you forgive men when they sin against you, your heavenly Father will also forgive you."

MATTHEW 6:14

Bear with each other and forgive whatever grievances you may have against one another. Forgive as the Lord forgave you.

COLOSSIANS 3:13

Peter came to Jesus and asked, "Lord, how many times shall I forgive my brother when he sins against me? Up to seven times?" Jesus answered, "I tell you, not seven times, but seventy-seven times."

MATTHEW 18:21–22

FREEDOM

The LORD sets prisoners free.

PSALM 146:7

It is for freedom that Christ has set us free. Stand firm, then, and do not let yourselves be burdened again by a yoke of slavery.

GALATIANS 5:1

The creation itself will be liberated from its bondage to decay and brought into the glorious freedom of the children of God.

ROMANS 8:21

The Lord is the Spirit, and where the Spirit of the Lord is, there is freedom.

2 CORINTHIANS 3:17

Jesus said, "You will know the truth, and the truth will set you free."

JOHN 8:32

Jesus said, "If the Son sets you free, you will be free indeed."

JOHN 8:36

Now that you have been set free from sin and have become slaves to God, the benefit you reap leads to holiness, and the result is eternal life.

ROMANS 6:22

Be sure of this: The wicked will not go unpunished, but those who are righteous will go free.

PROVERBS 11:21

Live as free men, but do not use your freedom as a cover-up for evil; live as servants of God.

I PETER 2:16

We know that our old self was crucified with [Christ] so that the body of sin might be done away with, that we should no longer be slaves to sin—because anyone who has died has been freed from sin.

ROMANS 6:6–7

Through Christ Jesus the law of the Spirit of life set me free from the law of sin and death.

ROMANS 8:2

FRIENDSHIP

As iron sharpens iron,
   so one man sharpens another.

PROVERBS 27:17

Two are better than one,
   because they have a good return for their work:
If one falls down,
   his friend can help him up.
But pity the man who falls
   and has no one to help him up!
Also, if two lie down together, they will keep warm.
   But how can one keep warm alone?
Though one may be overpowered,
   two can defend themselves.
A cord of three strands is not quickly broken.

ECCLESIASTES 4:9–12

Wounds from a friend can be trusted.

PROVERBS 27:6

A friend loves at all times,
   and a brother is born for adversity.

PROVERBS 17:17

Be devoted to one another in brotherly love. Honor one another above yourselves.

ROMANS 12:10

Jesus said, "Greater love has no one than this, that he lay down his life for his friends. You are my friends if you do what I command. I no longer call you servants, because a servant does not know his master's business. Instead, I have called you friends, for everything that I learned from my Father I have made known to you."

JOHN 15:13–15

A man of many companions may come to ruin,
but there is a friend who sticks closer than
a brother.

PROVERBS 18:24

Do not forsake your friend and the friend of your father.

PROVERBS 27:10

FUTURE

As it is written:
"No eye has seen,
no ear has heard,
no mind has conceived
what God has prepared for those who
love him"—
but God has revealed it to us by his Spirit.
The Spirit searches all things, even the deep things
of God.

1 CORINTHIANS 2:9–10

For the revelation awaits an appointed time;
it speaks of the end
and will not prove false.
Though it linger, wait for it;
it will certainly come and will not delay.

HABAKKUK 2:3

Listen, you who say, "Today or tomorrow we will
go to this or that city, spend a year there, carry on
business and make money." Why, you do not even
know what will happen tomorrow. What is your
life? You are a mist that appears for a little while
and then vanishes. Instead, you ought to say, "If it
is th Lord's will, we will live and do this or that."

JAMES 4:13–15

"I know the plans I have for you,"
declares the LORD, "plans to prosper
you and not to harm you, plans to
give you hope and a future."

JEREMIAH 29:11

*We are children of God, and what we will be has
not yet been made known. But we know that when
he appears, we shall be like him, for we shall see
him as he is.*

I JOHN 3:2

*Listen, I tell you a mystery: We will not all sleep,
but we will all be changed—in a flash, in the twinkling of an eye, at the last trumpet. For the trumpet
will sound, the dead will be raised imperishable, and
we will be changed.*

I CORINTHIANS 15:51–52

*Jesus said, "I say to all of you: In the future you will
see the Son of Man sitting at the right hand of the
Mighty One and coming on the clouds of heaven."*

MATTHEW 26:64

GENEROSITY

A generous man will himself be blessed,
for he shares his food with the poor.

PROVERBS 22:9

Good will come to him who is generous and
lends freely,
who conducts his affairs with justice.

PSALM 112:5

A generous man will prosper; he who refreshes others will himself be refreshed.

PROVERBS 11:25

Remember this: Whoever sows sparingly will also
reap sparingly, and whoever sows generously will
also reap generously.

2 CORINTHIANS 9:6

Command them to do good, to be rich in good
deeds, and to be generous and willing to share. In
this way they will lay up treasure for themselves as a
firm foundation for the coming age, so that they
may take hold of the life that is truly life.

1 TIMOTHY 6:18–19

The wicked borrow and do not repay,
but the righteous give generously.

PSALM 37:21

We have different gifts, according to the grace given us. If a man's gift is ... contributing to the needs of others, let him give generously.

ROMANS 12:6, 8

You will be made rich in every way so that you can be generous on every occasion, and through us your generosity will result in thanksgiving to God.

2 CORINTHIANS 9:11

I was young and now I am old,
yet I have never seen the righteous forsaken
or their children begging bread.
They are always generous and lend freely;
their children will be blessed.

PSALM 37:25–26

GENTLENESS

Jesus said, "Take my yoke upon you and learn from me, for I am gentle and humble in heart, and you will find rest for your souls."

MATTHEW 11:29

As God's chosen people, holy and dearly loved, clothe yourselves with compassion, kindness, humility, gentleness and patience.

COLOSSIANS 3:12

In your hearts set apart Christ as Lord. Always be prepared to give an answer to everyone who asks you to give the reason for the hope that you have. But do this with gentleness and respect.

1 PETER 3:15

The meek will inherit the land and enjoy great peace.

PSALM 37:11

The fruit of the Spirit is love, joy, peace, patience, kindness, goodness, faithfulness, gentleness and self-control. Against such things there is no law.

GALATIANS 5:22–23

A gentle answer turns away wrath.

PROVERBS 15:1

Pursue righteousness, godliness, faith, love, endurance and gentleness. Fight the good fight of the faith.

I TIMOTHY 6:11–12

Let your gentleness be evident to all. The Lord is near.

PHILIPPIANS 4:5

Be completely humble and gentle; be patient, bearing with one another in love.

EPHESIANS 4:2

If anyone sets his heart on being an overseer, he desires a noble task. Now the overseer must be above reproach, the husband of but one wife, temperate, self-controlled, respectable, hospitable, able to teach, not given to drunkenness, not violent but gentle, not quarrelsome, not a lover of money. He must manage his own family well and see that his children obey him with proper respect.

I TIMOTHY 3:1–4

GIVING

Jesus said, "Give to everyone who asks you."

LUKE 6:30

Jesus said, "Give, and it will be given to you. A good measure, pressed down, shaken together and running over, will be poured into your lap. For with the measure you use, it will be measured to you."

LUKE 6:38

Jesus said, "When you give to the needy, do not let your left hand know what your right hand is doing, so that your giving may be in secret. Then your Father, who sees what is done in secret, will reward you."

MATTHEW 6:3–4

Jesus said, "It is more blessed to give than to receive."

ACTS 20:35

If your enemy is hungry, give him food to eat;
*   if he is thirsty, give him water to drink.*

PROVERBS 25:21

Give generously to him and do so without a grudging heart; then because of this the LORD your God will bless you in all your work and in everything you put your hand to. There will always be poor people in the land. Therefore I command you to be openhanded toward your brothers and toward the poor and needy in your land.

DEUTERONOMY 15:10–11

"Bring the whole tithe into the storehouse, that there may be food in my house. Test me in this," says the LORD Almighty, "and see if I will not throw open the floodgates of heaven and pour out so much blessing that you will not have room enough for it."

MALACHI 3:10

Jesus said, "If you then, though you are evil, know how to give good gifts to your children, how much more will your Father in heaven give the Holy Spirit to those who ask him!"

LUKE 11:13

*He who gives to the poor will lack nothing,
    but he who closes his eyes to them receives
        many curses.*

PROVERBS 28:27

GOALS

Jesus said, "Seek first [God's] kingdom and his righteousness, and all these things will be given to you as well."

MATTHEW 6:33

We make it our goal to please [the Lord], whether we are at home in the body or away from it.

2 CORINTHIANS 5:9

Do you not know that in a race all the runners run, but only one gets the prize? Run in such a way as to get the prize.

1 CORINTHIANS 9:24

Brothers, I do not consider myself yet to have taken hold of it. But one thing I do: Forgetting what is behind and straining toward what is ahead, I press on toward the goal to win the prize for which God has called me heavenward in Christ Jesus.

PHILIPPIANS 3:13–14

Do your best to present yourself to God as one approved, a workman who does not need to be ashamed and who correctly handles the word of truth.

2 TIMOTHY 2:15

Follow the way of love and eagerly desire spiritual gifts, especially the gift of prophecy.

1 CORINTHIANS 14:1

Then Job replied to the LORD: "I know that you can do all things; no plan of yours can be thwarted."

JOB 42:1–2

Since you are eager to have spiritual gifts, try to excel in gifts that build up the church.

1 CORINTHIANS 14:12

If the LORD delights in a man's way, he makes his steps firm.

PSALM 37:23

Make it your ambition to lead a quiet life, to mind your own business and to work with your hands, just as we told you.

1 THESSALONIANS 4:11

GOD'S FAITHFULNESS

The LORD is faithful to all his promises
and loving toward all he has made.

PSALM 145:13

God, who has called you into fellowship with his Son Jesus Christ our Lord, is faithful.

1 CORINTHIANS 1:9

I will sing of the LORD's great love forever;
with my mouth I will make your
faithfulness known through all generations.
I will declare that your love stands firm forever,
that you established your faithfulness in
heaven itself.

PSALM 89:1–2

If we confess our sins, he is faithful and just and
will forgive us our sins and purify us from all
unrighteousness.

1 JOHN 1:9

Great is your love, [O LORD,] higher than the
heavens;
your faithfulness reaches to the skies.

PSALM 108:4

The LORD is good and his love endures forever;
his faithfulness continues through all
generations.

PSALM 100:5

The word of the LORD is right and true;
he is faithful in all he does.

PSALM 33:4

Know therefore that the LORD your God is God; he
is the faithful God, keeping his covenant of love to a
thousand generations of those who love him and
keep his commands.

DEUTERONOMY 7:9

All the ways of the LORD are loving
and faithful
for those who keep the demands
of his covenant.

PSALM 25:10

The Lord is faithful, and he will strengthen and pro-
tect you from the evil one.

2 THESSALONIANS 3:3

GOD'S LOVE

Many are the woes of the wicked,
but the LORD's unfailing love
surrounds the man who trusts in him.

PSALM 32:10

How great is the love the Father has lavished on us, that we should be called children of God! And that is what we are!

1 JOHN 3:1

As high as the heavens are above the earth,
so great is [God's] love for those who fear him.

PSALM 103:11

God is love. Whoever lives in love lives in God, and God in him. In this way, love is made complete among us so that we will have confidence on the day of judgment, because in this world we are like him.

1 JOHN 4:16–17

From everlasting to everlasting
the LORD's love is with those who fear him,
and his righteousness with their children's
children.

PSALM 103:17

Because of his great love for us, God, who is rich in mercy, made us alive with Christ even when we were dead in transgressions—it is by grace you have been saved.

EPHESIANS 2:4–5

I am convinced that neither death nor life, neither angels nor demons, neither the present nor the future, nor any powers, neither height nor depth, nor anything else in all creation, will be able to separate us from the love of God that is in Christ Jesus our Lord.

ROMANS 8:38–39

Jesus said, "He who loves me will be loved by my Father, and I too will love him and show myself to him."

JOHN 14:21

The LORD appeared to us in the past, saying:
"I have loved you with an everlasting love;
    I have drawn you with loving-kindness."

JEREMIAH 31:3

GOD'S MERCY

Praise be to the God and Father of our Lord Jesus Christ! In his great mercy he has given us new birth into a living hope through the resurrection of Jesus Christ from the dead.

1 PETER 1:3

[God] saved us, not because of righteous things we had done, but because of his mercy. He saved us through the washing of rebirth and renewal by the Holy Spirit.

TITUS 3:5

I, by your great mercy,
    will come into your house;
in reverence will I bow down
    toward your holy temple.

PSALM 5:7

*In [the LORD's] love and mercy he redeemed them;
    he lifted them up and carried them
    all the days of old.*

ISAIAH 63:9

Who is a God like you,
*   who pardons sin and forgives the transgression*
*   of the remnant of his inheritance?*
You do not stay angry forever
*   but delight to show mercy.*

MICAH 7:18

[God's] mercy extends to those
who fear him,
from generation to generation.

LUKE 1:50

Let the wicked forsake his way
*   and the evil man his thoughts.*
Let him turn to the LORD, and he will have mercy
*   on him,*
*   and to our God, for he will freely pardon.*

ISAIAH 55:7

Jesus said, "Be merciful, just as your Father is merciful."

LUKE 6:36

I urge you, brothers, in view of God's mercy, to offer your bodies as living sacrifices, holy and pleasing to God—this is your spiritual act of worship.

ROMANS 12:1

The LORD your God is a merciful God; he will not abandon or destroy you or forget the covenant with your forefathers, which he confirmed to them by oath.

DEUTERONOMY 4:31

"I am merciful," declares the LORD, "I will not be angry forever."

JEREMIAH 3:12

[Jesus] had to be made like his brothers in every way, in order that he might become a merciful and faithful high priest in service to God, and that he might make atonement for the sins of the people. Because he himself suffered when he was tempted, he is able to help those who are being tempted.

HEBREWS 2:17–18

Jesus said,
"Blessed are the merciful,
for they will be shown mercy."

MATTHEW 5:7

The Lord is full of compassion and mercy.

JAMES 5:11

Remember, O LORD, your great mercy and love,
for they are from of old.
Remember not the sins of my youth
and my rebellious ways;
according to your love remember me,
for you are good, O LORD.

PSALM 25:6–7

[God] says to Moses,
"I will have mercy on whom I have mercy,
and I will have compassion on whom I have
compassion."
It does not, therefore, depend on man's desire or
effort, but on God's mercy.

ROMANS 9:15–16

GOD'S PRESENCE

The LORD replied, "My Presence will go with you, and I will give you rest."

EXODUS 33:14

Blessed are those who have learned to acclaim you,
*   who walk in the light of your presence,*
*   O LORD.*

PSALM 89:15

Where can I go from your Spirit?
*   Where can I flee from your presence?*
If I go up to the heavens, you are there;
*   if I make my bed in the depths, you are there.*
If I rise on the wings of the dawn,
*   if I settle on the far side of the sea,*
even there your hand will guide me,
*   your right hand will hold me fast.*

PSALM 139:7–10

Jesus said, "Where two or three come together in my name, there am I with them."

MATTHEW 18:20

You have made known to me the path of life;
you will fill me with joy in your presence,
with eternal pleasures at your right hand.

PSALM 16:11

Tremble, O earth, at the presence of the Lord,
at the presence of the God of Jacob,
who turned the rock into a pool,
the hard rock into springs of water.

PSALM 114:7–8

This then is how we know that we belong to the truth, and how we set our hearts at rest in his presence whenever our hearts condemn us. For God is greater than our hearts, and he knows everything.

1 JOHN 3:19–20

In my integrity you uphold me
and set me in your presence forever.

PSALM 41:12

GOD'S WILL

You need to persevere so that when you have done the will of God, you will receive what he has promised.

HEBREWS 10:36

Do not conform any longer to the pattern of this world, but be transformed by the renewing of your mind. Then you will be able to test and approve what God's will is—his good, pleasing and perfect will.

ROMANS 12:2

In him we were also chosen, having been predestined according to the plan of him who works out everything in conformity with the purpose of his will, in order that we, who were the first to hope in Christ, might be for the praise of his glory.

EPHESIANS 1:11–12

The world and its desires pass away, but the man who does the will of God lives forever.

1 JOHN 2:17

Jesus said, "My Father's will is that everyone who looks to the Son and believes in him shall have eternal life, and I will raise him up at the last day."

JOHN 6:40

[God] made known to us the mystery of his will according to his good pleasure, which he purposed in Christ, to be put into effect when the times will have reached their fulfillment—to bring all things in heaven and on earth together under one head, even Christ.

EPHESIANS 1:9–10

[God] listens to the godly man who does his will.

JOHN 9:31

[God] who searches our hearts knows the mind of the Spirit, because the Spirit intercedes for the saints in accordance with God's will.

ROMANS 8:27

Jesus said, "Whoever does God's will is my brother and sister and mother."

MARK 3:35

Be joyful always; pray continually; give thanks in all circumstances, for this is God's will for you in Christ Jesus.

1 THESSALONIANS 5:16–18

GOD'S WORD

*The word of God is living and active. Sharper than
any double-edged sword, it penetrates even to dividing soul and spirit, joints and marrow; it judges the
thoughts and attitudes of the heart.*

HEBREWS 4:12

*The unfolding of your words gives light;
    it gives understanding to the simple.*

PSALM 119:130

*You have been born again, not of perishable seed,
but of imperishable, through the living and enduring
word of God. For,
"All men are like grass,
    and all their glory is like the flowers of the field;
the grass withers and the flowers fall,
    but the word of the Lord stands forever."*

1 PETER 1:23–25

Your word, O LORD, is eternal;
it stands firm in the heavens.

PSALM 119:89

Jesus said, "Heaven and earth will pass away, but my words will never pass away."

MARK 13:31

Every word of God is flawless;
he is a shield to those who take refuge in him.

PROVERBS 30:5

I will bow down toward your holy temple
and will praise your name
for your love and your faithfulness,
for you have exalted above all things
your name and your word.

PSALM 138:2

All Scripture is God-breathed and is useful for teaching, rebuking, correcting and training in righteousness, so that the man of God may be thoroughly equipped for every good work.

2 TIMOTHY 3:16–17

GOODNESS

Do not forget to do good and to share with others, for with such sacrifices God is pleased.

HEBREWS 13:16

Test everything. Hold on to the good. Avoid every kind of evil.

1 THESSALONIANS 5:21–22

Trust in the LORD and do good;
dwell in the land and enjoy safe pasture.

PSALM 37:3

Anyone who does what is good is from God.

3 JOHN v.11

We are God's workmanship, created in Christ Jesus to do good works, which God prepared in advance for us to do.

EPHESIANS 2:10

I know that there is nothing better for men than to be happy and do good while they live.

ECCLESIASTES 3:12

Jesus said, "Let your light shine before men, that
they may see your good deeds and praise your
Father in heaven."

MATTHEW 5:16

As we have opportunity, let us do good to all
people, especially to those who belong to the family
of believers.

GALATIANS 6:10

Surely goodness and love will follow me
    all the days of my life,
and I will dwell in the house of the LORD
    forever.

PSALM 23:6

How great is your goodness,
which you have stored up for
those who fear you.

PSALM 31:19

Turn from evil and do good;
    then you will dwell in the land forever.

PSALM 37:27

GRACE

From the fullness of his grace we have all received one blessing after another.

JOHN 1:16

It is by grace you have been saved, through faith— and this not from yourselves, it is the gift of God— not by works, so that no one can boast. For we are God's workmanship, created in Christ Jesus to do good works, which God prepared in advance for us to do.

EPHESIANS 2:8–10

You know the grace of our Lord Jesus Christ, that though he was rich, yet for your sakes he became poor, so that you through his poverty might become rich.

2 CORINTHIANS 8:9

Grace and peace be yours in abundance through the knowledge of God and of Jesus our Lord.

2 PETER 1:2

Let us then approach the throne of grace with confidence, so that we may receive mercy and find grace to help us in our time of need.

HEBREWS 4:16

[The LORD] gives grace to the humble.

PROVERBS 3:34

[God] has saved us and called us to a holy life—not because of anything we have done but because of his own purpose and grace. This grace was given us in Christ Jesus before the beginning of time.

2 TIMOTHY 1:9

[The Lord] said to me, "My grace is sufficient for you, for my power is made perfect in weakness." Therefore I will boast all the more gladly about my weaknesses, so that Christ's power may rest on me.

2 CORINTHIANS 12:9

God is able to make all grace abound to you, so that in all things at all times, having all that you need, you will abound in every good work.

2 CORINTHIANS 9:8

GRIEF

When my heart was grieved
   and my spirit embittered,
I was senseless and ignorant;
   I was a brute beast before you.
Yet I am always with you;
   you hold me by my right hand.

PSALM 73:21–23

Jesus said, "I tell you the truth, you will weep and mourn while the world rejoices. You will grieve, but your grief will turn to joy."

JOHN 16:20

The LORD is close to the brokenhearted
   and saves those who are crushed in spirit.

PSALM 34:18

Remember your word to your servant,
   for you have given me hope.
My comfort in my suffering is this:
   Your promise preserves my life.

PSALM 119:49–50

The ransomed of the LORD will return.
They will enter Zion with singing;
everlasting joy will crown their heads.
Gladness and joy will overtake them,
and sorrow and sighing will flee away.

ISAIAH 35:10

Jesus said,
"Blessed are those who mourn,
for they will be comforted."

MATTHEW 5:4

The Spirit of the Sovereign LORD ...
has sent me to bind up the brokenhearted, ...
to comfort all who mourn,
and provide for those who grieve
in Zion— ...
the oil of gladness
instead of mourning,
and a garment of praise
instead of a spirit of despair.

ISAIAH 61:1–3

GUIDANCE

I will instruct you and teach you in
the way you should go;
I will counsel you and watch
over you.

PSALM 32:8

*Jesus said, "When he, the Spirit of truth, comes, he
will guide you into all truth. He will not speak on
his own; he will speak only what he hears, and he
will tell you what is yet to come."*

JOHN 16:13

Whether you turn to the right or to
the left, your ears will hear a voice
behind you, saying, "This is the way;
walk in it."

ISAIAH 30:21

Good and upright is the LORD;
    therefore he instructs sinners in his ways.
He guides the humble in what is right
    and teaches them his way.

PSALM 25:8–9

The LORD *is my shepherd, I shall not be in want.*
He makes me lie down in green pastures,
he leads me beside quiet waters,
he restores my soul.
He guides me in paths of righteousness
for his name's sake.

PSALM 23:1–3

The LORD *will guide you always;*
he will satisfy your needs in a sun-scorched land
and will strengthen your frame.
You will be like a well-watered garden,
like a spring whose waters never fail.

ISAIAH 58:11

If I rise on the wings of the dawn,
if I settle on the far side of the sea,
even there your hand will guide me,
your right hand will hold me fast.

PSALM 139:9–10

GUILT

Repent, then, and turn to God, so that your sins may be wiped out, that times of refreshing may come from the Lord, and that he may send the Christ, who has been appointed for you—even Jesus.

ACTS 3:19–20

Turn from evil and do good;
*   then you will dwell in the land forever.*

PSALM 37:27

My dear children, I write this to you so that you will not sin. But if anybody does sin, we have one who speaks to the Father in our defense—Jesus Christ, the Righteous One.

I JOHN 2:1

Let us draw near to God with a sincere heart in full assurance of faith, having our hearts sprinkled to cleanse us from a guilty conscience and having our bodies washed with pure water.

HEBREWS 10:22

Godly sorrow brings repentance that leads to salvation and leaves no regret.

2 CORINTHIANS 7:10

Jesus said, "I tell you, there is rejoicing in the presence of the angels of God over one sinner who repents."

LUKE 15:10

Praise the LORD....
He provided redemption for his people;
    he ordained his covenant forever—
    holy and awesome is his name.

PSALM 111:1, 9

Jesus said, "I tell you that ... there will be more rejoicing in heaven over one sinner who repents than over ninety-nine righteous persons who do not need to repent."

LUKE 15:7

If a wicked man turns away from all the sins he has committed and keeps all my decrees and does what is just and right, he will surely live; he will not die. None of the offenses he has committed will be remembered against him. Because of the righteous things he has done, he will live.

EZEKIEL 18:21–22

There is now no condemnation for those who are in Christ Jesus, because through Christ Jesus the law of the Spirit of life set me free from the law of sin and death. For what the law was powerless to do in that it was weakened by the sinful nature, God did by sending his own Son in the likeness of sinful man to be a sin offering.

ROMANS 8:1–3

Create in me a pure heart, O God, and renew a steadfast spirit within me.

PSALM 51:10

This is what the LORD says: "I will cleanse them from all the sin they have committed against me and will forgive all their sins of rebellion against me."

JEREMIAH 33:8

Christ loved the church and gave himself up for her to make her holy, cleansing her by the washing with water through the word, and to present her to himself as a radiant church, without stain or wrinkle or any other blemish, but holy and blameless.

EPHESIANS 5:25–27

"I have swept away your offenses like a cloud,
your sins like the morning mist.
Return to me,
for I have redeemed you," says the LORD.

ISAIAH 44:22

God has rescued us from the dominion of darkness
and brought us into the kingdom of the Son he
loves, in whom we have redemption, the forgiveness
of sins.

COLOSSIANS 1:13–14

It was not with perishable things such as silver or
gold that you were redeemed from the empty way of
life handed down to you from your forefathers, but
with the precious blood of Christ, a lamb without
blemish or defect.

I PETER 1:18–19

Put your hope in the LORD,
for with the LORD is unfailing love
and with him is full redemption.

PSALM 130:7

HAPPINESS

To the man who pleases him, God gives wisdom, knowledge and happiness.

ECCLESIASTES 2:26

May the righteous be glad and rejoice before God; may they be happy and joyful.

PSALM 68:3

A happy heart makes the face cheerful, but heartache crushes the spirit.

PROVERBS 15:13

I know that there is nothing better for men than to be happy and do good while they live.

ECCLESIASTES 3:12

When God gives any man wealth and possessions, and enables him to enjoy them, to accept his lot and be happy in his work—this is a gift of God.

ECCLESIASTES 5:19

I commend the enjoyment of life, because nothing is better for a man under the sun than to eat and drink and be glad. Then joy will accompany him in his work all the days of the life God has given him under the sun.

ECCLESIASTES 8:15

When times are good, be happy; but when times are bad, consider: God has made the one as well as the other.

ECCLESIASTES 7:14

Be glad, O people of Zion,
rejoice in the LORD your God,
for he has given you
the autumn rains in righteousness.
He sends you abundant showers,
both autumn and spring rains, as before.

JOEL 2:23

HEALTH & HEALING

The LORD says, "I will heal my people and will let them enjoy abundant peace and security."

JEREMIAH 33:6

A heart at peace gives life to the body.

PROVERBS 14:30

O LORD my God, I called to you for help
*   and you healed me.*
O LORD, you brought me up from the grave;
*   you spared me from going down into the pit.*

PSALM 30:2–3

"I will restore you to health
*   and heal your wounds," declares the Lord.*

JEREMIAH 30:17

[The LORD said,] "I am the LORD, who heals you."

EXODUS 15:26

A cheerful look brings joy to the heart,
*   and good news gives health to the bones.*

PROVERBS 15:30

Do not be wise in your own eyes;
    fear the LORD and shun evil.
This will bring health to your body
    and nourishment to your bones.

PROVERBS 3:7–8

The prayer offered in faith will make the sick person
well; the Lord will raise him up.

JAMES 5:15

Praise the LORD, O my soul,
    and forget not all his benefits—
who forgives all your sins
    and heals all your diseases.

PSALM 103:2–3

He himself bore our sins in his body on the tree, so
that we might die to sins and live for righteousness;
by his wounds you have been healed.

1 PETER 2:24

HEAVEN

Jesus said, "In my Father's house are many rooms; if it were not so, I would have told you. I am going there to prepare a place for you. And if I go and prepare a place for you, I will come back and take you to be with me that you also may be where I am."

JOHN 14:2–3

The throne of God and of the Lamb will be in the city, and his servants will serve him. They will see his face, and his name will be on their foreheads. There will be no more night. They will not need the light of a lamp or the light of the sun, for the Lord God will give them light. And they will reign for ever and ever.

REVELATION 22:3–5

God himself will be with them and be their God. He will wipe every tear from their eyes. There will be no more death or mourning or crying or pain, for the old order of things has passed away.

REVELATION 21:3–4

Surely goodness and love will follow me
  all the days of my life,
and I will dwell in the house of the LORD
  forever.

PSALM 23:6

The Lord himself will come down from heaven,
with a loud command, with the voice of the
archangel and with the trumpet call of God, and the
dead in Christ will rise first. After that, we who are
still alive and are left will be caught up together
with them in the clouds to meet the Lord in the air.
And so we will be with the Lord forever.

1 THESSALONIANS 4:16–17

**If the earthly tent we live in is
destroyed, we have a building from
God, an eternal house in heaven, not
built by human hands.**

2 CORINTHIANS 5:1

Never again will they hunger;
*   never again will they thirst.*
The sun will not beat upon them,
*   nor any scorching heat.*
For the Lamb at the center of the throne will be
*   their shepherd;*
*   he will lead them to springs of living water.*
And God will wipe away every tear from their eyes.

REVELATION 7:16–17

HELP

So we say with confidence,
  "The Lord is my helper; I will not be afraid.
  What can man do to me?"

HEBREWS 13:6

Because he himself suffered when he was tempted, he is able to help those who are being tempted.

HEBREWS 2:18

It is the Sovereign LORD who helps me.
  Who is he that will condemn me?
They will all wear out like a garment;
  the moths will eat them up.

ISAIAH 50:9

We wait in hope for the LORD;
  he is our help and our shield.

PSALM 33:20

The LORD is my strength and my shield;
  my heart trusts in him, and I am helped.
My heart leaps for joy
  and I will give thanks to him in song.

PSALM 28:7

God is our refuge and strength,
  an ever-present help in trouble.

PSALM 46:1

[God] will deliver the needy who cry out,
  the afflicted who have no one to help.

PSALM 72:12

The victim commits himself to you;
  you are the helper of the fatherless.

PSALM 10:14

The Spirit helps us in our weakness.
We do not know what we ought to
pray for, but the Spirit himself intercedes for us with groans that words
cannot express.

ROMANS 8:26

HOLY SPIRIT

The Lord is the Spirit, and where the Spirit of the Lord is, there is freedom.

2 CORINTHIANS 3:17

Peter said, "Repent and be baptized, every one of you, in the name of Jesus Christ for the forgiveness of your sins. And you will receive the gift of the Holy Spirit. The promise is for you and your children and for all who are far off—for all whom the Lord our God will call."

ACTS 2:38–39

"I will pour out my Spirit on all people.
Your sons and daughters will prophesy,
   your old men will dream dreams,
   your young men will see visions.
Even on my servants, both men and women,
   I will pour out my Spirit," says the LORD.

JOEL 2:28–29

You also were included in Christ when you heard the word of truth, the gospel of your salvation. Having believed, you were marked in him with a seal, the promised Holy Spirit, who is a deposit guaranteeing our inheritance until the redemption of those who are God's possession.

　　　　EPHESIANS 1:13–14

Do not believe every spirit, but test the spirits to see whether they are from God. . . . This is how you can recognize the Spirit of God: Every spirit that acknowledges that Jesus Christ has come in the flesh is from God.

1 JOHN 4:1–2

Jesus said, "I will ask the Father, and he will give you another Counselor to be with you forever—the Spirit of truth. The world cannot accept him, because it neither sees him nor knows him. But you know him, for he lives with you and will be in you."

JOHN 14:16–17

We have not received the spirit of the world but the Spirit who is from God, that we may understand what God has freely given us.

1 CORINTHIANS 2:12

If the Spirit of him who raised Jesus from the dead is living in you, he who raised Christ from the dead will also give life to your mortal bodies through his Spirit, who lives in you.

ROMANS 8:11

HONESTY

Whoever of you loves life
and desires to see many
good days,
keep your tongue from evil
and your lips from speaking lies.

PSALM 34:12–13

Kings take pleasure in honest lips;
they value a man who speaks the truth.

PROVERBS 16:13

He who walks righteously
and speaks what is right,
who rejects gain from extortion
and keeps his hand from accepting bribes,
who stops his ears against plots of murder
and shuts his eyes against contemplating evil—
this is the man who will dwell on the heights,
whose refuge will be the mountain fortress.
His bread will be supplied,
and water will not fail him.

ISAIAH 33:15–16

An honest answer
is like a kiss on the lips.

PROVERBS 24:26

A truthful witness gives honest testimony.

PROVERBS 12:17

Whatever is true, whatever is noble, whatever is right, whatever is pure, whatever is lovely, whatever is admirable—if anything is excellent or praiseworthy—think about such things.

PHILIPPIANS 4:8

Truthful lips endure forever.

PROVERBS 12:19

The LORD detests lying lips,
but he delights in men who are truthful.

PROVERBS 12:22

HOPE

The eyes of the LORD are on those who fear him,
on those whose hope is in his unfailing love.

PSALM 33:18

May the God of hope fill you with all joy and peace
as you trust in him, so that you may overflow with
hope by the power of the Holy Spirit.

ROMANS 15:13

Those who hope in the LORD
will renew their strength.
They will soar on wings like eagles;
they will run and not grow weary,
they will walk and not be faint.

ISAIAH 40:31

We have put our hope in the living God, who is the Savior of all men, and especially of those who believe.

1 TIMOTHY 4:10

Know also that wisdom is sweet to your soul;
if you find it, there is a future hope for you,
and your hope will not be cut off.

PROVERBS 24:14

No one whose hope is in you will ever be put to shame.

PSALM 25:3

Blessed is he whose help is the God of Jacob,
*   whose hope is in the LORD his God,*
the Maker of heaven and earth,
*   the sea, and everything in them—*
*   the LORD, who remains faithful forever.*

PSALM 146:5–6

We rejoice in the hope of the glory of God. Not only so, but we also rejoice in our sufferings, because we know that suffering produces perseverance; perseverance, character; and character, hope. And hope does not disappoint us, because God has poured out his love into our hearts by the Holy Spirit, whom he has given us.

ROMANS 5:2–5

Set your hope fully on the grace to be given you when Jesus Christ is revealed.

1 PETER 1:13

HUMILITY

*Jesus said, "The greatest among you will be your
servant. For whoever exalts himself will be humbled,
and whoever humbles himself will be exalted."*

MATTHEW 23:11–12

*Do not think of yourself more highly than you
ought, but rather think of yourself with sober judgment, in accordance with the measure of faith God
has given you.*

ROMANS 12:3

Humility and the fear of the LORD
bring wealth and honor and life.

PROVERBS 22:4

*Clothe yourselves with humility toward one
another, because,*

> *"God opposes the proud
>   but gives grace to the humble."*

*Humble yourselves, therefore, under God's mighty
hand, that he may lift you up in due time.*

1 PETER 5:5–6

The LORD takes delight in his people;
  he crowns the humble with salvation.

PSALM 149:4

Humble yourselves before the Lord, and he will lift you up.

JAMES 4:10

The LORD sustains the humble
  but casts the wicked to the ground.

PSALM 147:6

A man's pride brings him low,
  but a man of lowly spirit gains honor.

PROVERBS 29:23

He guides the humble in what is right and teaches them his way.

PSALM 25:9

You, [O LORD,] save the humble,
  but your eyes are on the haughty to bring
    them low.

2 SAMUEL 22:28

IDENTITY

*You are a chosen people, a royal priesthood, a holy
nation, a people belonging to God, that you may
declare the praises of him who called you out of
darkness into his wonderful light.*

1 PETER 2:9

*Know that the LORD is God.
It is he who made us, and we are his;
we are his people, the sheep of his pasture.*

PSALM 100:3

We are God's workmanship, created in Christ Jesus to do good works, which God prepared in advance for us to do.

EPHESIANS 2:10

*Now, this is what the LORD says . . .
"Fear not, for I have redeemed you;
I have summoned you by name; you are mine."*

ISAIAH 43:1

"Before I formed you in the womb I
knew you,
before you were born I set you
apart," says the LORD.

JEREMIAH 1:5

*You also were included in Christ when you heard
the word of truth, the gospel of your salvation.
Having believed, you were marked in him with a
seal, the promised Holy Spirit, who is a deposit
guaranteeing our inheritance until the redemption of
those who are God's possession.*

EPHESIANS 1:13–14

*Come, let us bow down in worship,
 let us kneel before the LORD our Maker;
for he is our God
 and we are the people of his pasture,
 the flock under his care.*

PSALM 95:6–7

INTEGRITY

The LORD God is a sun and shield;
the LORD bestows favor and honor;
no good thing does he withhold
from those whose walk is blameless.

PSALM 84:11

The integrity of the upright guides them.

PROVERBS 11:3

I know, my God, that you test the heart and are
pleased with integrity.

1 CHRONICLES 29:17

The man of integrity walks securely.

PROVERBS 10:9

Jesus said, "Whoever can be trusted with very little can also be trusted with much, and whoever is dishonest with very little will also be dishonest with much."

LUKE 16:10

Those who walk uprightly enter into peace.

ISAIAH 57:2

He holds victory in store for the upright,
  he is a shield to those whose walk is blameless,
for he guards the course of the just
  and protects the way of his faithful ones.

PROVERBS 2:7–8

Righteousness guards the man of integrity.

PROVERBS 13:6

In my integrity you uphold me and set me in your presence forever.

PSALM 41:12

The righteous man leads a blameless life;
  blessed are his children after him.

PROVERBS 20:7

JESUS CHRIST

The angel said to her, "... Mary, you have found favor with God. You will be with child and give birth to a son, and you are to give him the name Jesus. He will be great and will be called the Son of the Most High." ... "How will this be," Mary asked the angel, "since I am a virgin?" The angel answered, "The Holy Spirit will come upon you, and the power of the Most High will overshadow you. So the holy one to be born will be called the Son of God."

LUKE 1:30–32, 34–35

Christ was sacrificed once to take away the sins of many people; and he will appear a second time, not to bear sin, but to bring salvation to those who are waiting for him.

HEBREWS 9:28

Jesus Christ is the same yesterday and today and forever.

HEBREWS 13:8

In Christ all the fullness of the Deity lives in bodily form, and you have been given fullness in Christ, who is the head over every power and authority.

COLOSSIANS 2:9–10

*Our citizenship is in heaven. And we eagerly await a
Savior from there, the Lord Jesus Christ, who, by
the power that enables him to bring everything
under his control, will transform our lowly bodies
so that they will be like his glorious body.*

PHILIPPIANS 3:20–21

[Jesus Christ] is the atoning sacrifice
for our sins, and not only for ours but
also for the sins of the whole world.

1 JOHN 2:2

*Christ is the mediator of a new covenant, that those
who are called may receive the promised eternal
inheritance—now that he has died as a ransom to
set them free from the sins committed under the
first covenant.*

HEBREWS 9:15

This is how we know what love is:
Jesus Christ laid down his life for us.

1 JOHN 3:16

JOY

The joy of the LORD is your strength.

NEHEMIAH 8:10

Consider it pure joy, my brothers, whenever you face trails of many kinds, because you know that the testing of your faith develops perseverance.

JAMES 1:2–3

The LORD your God will bless you in all your harvest and in all the work of your hands, and your joy will be complete.

DEUTERONOMY 16:15

Let all who take refuge in you be glad, [O LORD]; let them ever sing for joy.

PSALM 5:11

You turned my wailing into dancing; you removed my sackcloth and clothed me with joy, that my heart may sing to you and not be silent. O LORD my God, I will give you thanks forever.

PSALM 30:11–12

You have made known to me the path of life;
you will fill me with joy in your presence,
with eternal pleasures at your right hand.

PSALM 16:11

Those who sow in tears
will reap with songs of joy.

PSALM 126:5

Though you have not seen [Jesus], you love him;
and even though you do not see him now, you
believe in him and are filled with an inexpressible
and glorious joy, for you are receiving the goal of
your faith, the salvation of your souls.

1 PETER 1:8–9

The precepts of the LORD are right,
giving joy to the heart.

PSALM 19:8

Surely you have granted [the king] eternal blessings
and made him glad with the joy of your presence,
[O LORD].

PSALM 21:6

Your statutes are my heritage forever, [O LORD];
  they are the joy of my heart.

PSALM 119:111

The LORD declares,
"You will go out in joy
    and be led forth in peace;
the mountains and hills
    will burst into song before you,
and all the trees of the field
    will clap their hands."

ISAIAH 55:12

Jesus said, "Until now you have not asked for any-
thing in my name. Ask and you will receive, and
your joy will be complete."

JOHN 16:24

[God] will yet fill your mouth with laughter
  and your lips with shouts of joy.

JOB 8:21

*You make me glad by your deeds, O L*ORD;
I sing for joy at the works of your hands.

PSALM 92:4

Tremble before him, all the earth!
The world is firmly established; it cannot
be moved.
Let the heavens rejoice, let the earth be glad;
let them say among the nations,
*"The L*ORD *reigns!"*
Let the sea resound, and all that is in it;
let the fields be jubilant, and everything in them!
Then the trees of the forest will sing,
*they will sing for joy before the L*ORD,
for he comes to judge the earth.

1 CHRONICLES 16:30–33

Light is shed upon the righteous and joy on the upright in heart.

PSALM 97:11

JUSTICE

[The LORD] has showed you, O man, what is good.
And what does the LORD require of you?
To act justly and to love mercy
and to walk humbly with your God.

MICAH 6:8

The LORD is righteous,
he loves justice;
upright men will see his face.

PSALM 11:7

The LORD is known by his justice;
the wicked are ensnared by the work of
their hands.

PSALM 9:16

Many seek an audience with a ruler,
but it is from the LORD that man gets justice.

PROVERBS 29:26

God's judgment is right, and as a result you will be counted worthy of the kingdom of God.

2 THESSALONIANS 1:5

The LORD is a God of justice.
   Blessed are all who wait for him!

ISAIAH 30:18

Speak up for those who cannot speak for themselves,
   for the rights of all who are destitute.
Speak up and judge fairly;
   defend the rights of the poor and needy.

PROVERBS 31:8–9

Learn to do right!
Seek justice,
   encourage the oppressed.
Defend the case of the fatherless,
   plead the case of the widow.

ISAIAH 1:17

KINDNESS

As God's chosen people, holy and dearly loved, clothe yourselves with compassion, kindness, humility, gentleness and patience.

COLOSSIANS 3:12

Make sure that nobody pays back wrong for wrong, but always try to be kind to each other and to everyone else.

1 THESSALONIANS 5:15

Whoever is kind to the needy honors God.

PROVERBS 14:31

Jesus said, "In everything, do to others what you would have them do to you, for this sums up the Law and the Prophets."

MATTHEW 7:12

When the kindness and love of God our Savior appeared, he saved us, not because of righteous things we had done, but because of his mercy.

TITUS 3:4–5

He who is kind to the poor lends to the LORD,
and he will reward him for what he has done.

PROVERBS 19:17

A kind man benefits himself,
but a cruel man brings trouble
on himself.

PROVERBS 11:17

Be kind and compassionate to one another, forgiving
each other, just as in Christ God forgave you. Be
imitators of God, therefore, as dearly loved children
and live a life of love, just as Christ loved us and
gave himself up for us as a fragrant offering and sac-
rifice to God.

EPHESIANS 4:32—5:2

Make every effort to add to your faith goodness;
and to goodness, knowledge; and to knowledge,
self-control; and to self-control, perseverance; and to
perseverance, godliness; and to godliness, brotherly
kindness; and to brotherly kindness, love.

2 PETER 1:5–7

KINGDOM OF GOD

[God] has rescued us from the dominion of darkness and brought us into the kingdom of the Son he loves, in whom we have redemption, the forgiveness of sins.

COLOSSIANS 1:13–14

The kingdom of God is not a matter of eating and drinking, but of righteousness, peace and joy in the Holy Spirit, because anyone who serves Christ in this way is pleasing to God and approved by men.

ROMANS 14:17–18

The LORD has established his throne in heaven, and his kingdom rules over all.

PSALM 103:19

Since we are receiving a kingdom that cannot be shaken, let us be thankful, and so worship God acceptably with reverence and awe.

HEBREWS 12:28

"I tell you the truth," Jesus said to them, "no one who has left home or wife or brothers or parents or children for the sake of the kingdom of God will fail to receive many times as much in this age and, in the age to come, eternal life."

LUKE 18:29–30

Jesus said, "Do not be afraid, little flock, for your Father has been pleased to give you the kingdom."

LUKE 12:32

All you have made will praise you, O LORD;
your saints will extol you.
They will tell of the glory of your kingdom
and speak of your might,
so that all men may know of your mighty acts
and the glorious splendor of your kingdom.
Your kingdom is an everlasting kingdom,
and your dominion endures through all
generations.

PSALM 145:10–13

KNOWLEDGE

This is my prayer: that your love may abound more and more in knowledge and depth of insight, so that you may be able to discern what is best and may be pure and blameless until the day of Christ.

PHILIPPIANS 1:9–10

Grace and peace be yours in abundance through the knowledge of God and of Jesus our Lord. His divine power has given us everything we need for life and godliness through our knowledge of him who called us by his own glory and goodness.

2 PETER 1:2–3

The prudent are crowned with knowledge.

PROVERBS 14:18

To the man who pleases him, God gives wisdom, knowledge and happiness, but to the sinner he gives the task of gathering and storing up wealth to hand it over to the one who pleases God.

ECCLESIASTES 2:26

Grow in the grace and knowledge of our Lord and Savior Jesus Christ.

2 PETER 3:18

*God, who said, "Let light shine out of darkness,"
made his light shine in our hearts to give us the
light of the knowledge of the glory of God in the
face of Christ.*

Since the day we heard about you,
we have not stopped praying for you
and asking God to fill you with the
knowledge of his will through all
spiritual wisdom and understanding.

2 CORINTHIANS 1:9

*Gold there is, and rubies in abundance,
     but lips that speak knowledge are a rare jewel.*

PROVERBS 20:15

*Thanks be to God, who always leads us in tri-
umphal procession in Christ and through us spreads
everywhere the fragrance of the knowledge of him.*

2 CORINTHIANS 2:14

Knowledge of the Holy One is understanding.

PROVERBS 9:10

LEADERSHIP

"I will choose you ... and bring you to Zion. Then I will give you shepherds after my own heart, who will lead you with knowledge and understanding," declares the LORD.

JEREMIAH 3:14–15

The LORD said, "Be strong and coura-geous, because you will lead these people to inherit the land I swore to their forefathers to give them."

JOSHUA 1:6

In your unfailing love you will lead
   the people you have redeemed.
In your strength you will guide them
   to your holy dwelling.

EXODUS 15:13

We have different gifts, according to the grace given us. If a man's gift is ... serving, let him serve; if it is teaching, let him teach; if it is encouraging, let him encourage; if it is contributing to the needs of others, let him give generously; if it is leadership, let him govern diligently; if it is showing mercy, let him do it cheerfully.

ROMANS 12:6–8

Kings detest wrongdoing, for a throne is established through righteousness.

PROVERBS 16:12

Jesus said, "The greatest among you should be like the youngest, and the one who rules like the one who serves."

LUKE 22:26

Love and faithfulness keep a king safe; through love his throne is made secure.

PROVERBS 20:28

You will not leave in haste or go in flight; for the LORD will go before you, the God of Israel will be your rear guard.

ISAIAH 52:12

By justice a king gives a country stability, but one who is greedy for bribes tears it down.

PROVERBS 29:4

LIFE

Jesus said, "The Spirit gives life; the flesh counts for nothing. The words I have spoken to you are spirit and they are life."

JOHN 6:63

Set your hearts on things above, where Christ is seated at the right hand of God. Set your minds on things above, not on earthly things. For you died, and your life is now hidden with Christ in God. When Christ, who is your life, appears, then you also will appear with him in glory.

COLOSSIANS 3:1–4

With you, [O LORD,] is the fountain of life;
in your light we see light.

PSALM 36:9

Listen, my son, accept what I say,
and the years of your life will be many.

PROVERBS 4:10

Jesus said, "I have come that they may have life, and have it to the full."

JOHN 10:10

You have made known to me the paths of life;
    you will fill me with joy in your presence.

ACTS 2:28

Choose life, so that you and your children may live.
... For the LORD is your life, and he will give you
many years in the land he swore to give to your
fathers, Abraham, Isaac and Jacob.

DEUTERONOMY 30:19–20

Jesus declared, "I am the bread of life. He who
comes to me will never go hungry, and he who
believes in me will never be thirsty."

JOHN 6:35

The fear of the LORD adds length to life.

PROVERBS 10:27

If the Spirit of him who raised Jesus from the dead
is living in you, he who raised Christ from the dead
will also give life to your mortal bodies through his
Spirit, who lives in you.

ROMANS 8:11

LOVE

Jesus said, "Love your enemies, do good to them, and lend to them without expecting to get anything back. Then your reward will be great, and you will be sons of the Most High."

LUKE 6:35

Above all, love each other deeply, because love covers over a multitude of sins.

1 PETER 4:8

No one has ever seen God; but if we love one another, God lives in us and his love is made complete in us.

1 JOHN 4:12

Love the LORD your God with all your heart and with all your soul and with all your strength.

DEUTERONOMY 6:5

If anyone acknowledges that Jesus is the Son of God, God lives in him and he in God. And so we know and rely on the love God has for us. God is love. Whoever lives in love lives in God, and God in him.

1 JOHN 4:15–16

I pray that you, being rooted and established in love, may have power, together with all the saints, to grasp how wide and long and high and deep is the love of Christ, and to know this love that surpasses knowledge—that you may be filled to the measure of all the fullness of God.

EPHESIANS 3:17–19

If you really keep the royal law found in Scripture, "Love your neighbor as yourself," you are doing right.

JAMES 2:8

We love because he first loved us.

1 JOHN 4:19

Dear friends, let us love one another, for love comes from God. Everyone who loves has been born of God and knows God.

1 JOHN 4:7

This is love: not that we loved God, but that he loved us and sent his Son as an atoning sacrifice for our sins.

1 JOHN 4:10

MEDITATION

Let me understand the teaching of your precepts,
        [O LORD];
    then I will meditate on your wonders.

PSALM 119:27

**I will meditate on your works, [O God,]
and consider all your mighty deeds.**

PSALM 77:12

Blessed is the man
    who does not walk in the counsel of the wicked
or stand in the way of sinners
    or sit in the seat of mockers.
But his delight is in the law of the LORD,
    and on his law he meditates day and night.

PSALM 1:1–2

I rise before dawn and cry for help;
    I have put my hope in your word.
My eyes stay open through the watches of the night,
    that I may meditate on your promises.

PSALM 119:147–148

Do not let this Book of the Law depart from your
mouth; meditate on it day and night, so that you
may be careful to do everything written in it. Then
you will be prosperous and successful.

JOSHUA 1:8

Oh, how I love your law!
I meditate on it all day long.
Your commands make me wiser than my enemies,
for they are ever with me.
I have more insight than all my teachers,
for I meditate on your statutes.

PSALM 119:97–99

May the words of my mouth and the
meditation of my heart
be pleasing in your sight,
O LORD, my Rock and my
Redeemer.

PSALM 19:14

MINISTRY

It was [Christ] who gave some to be apostles, some to be prophets, some to be evangelists, and some to be pastors and teachers, to prepare God's people for works of service, so that the body of Christ may be built up until we all reach unity in the faith and in the knowledge of the Son of God and become mature, attaining to the whole measure of the fullness of Christ.

EPHESIANS 4:11–13

Serve wholeheartedly, as if you were serving the Lord, not men, because you know that the Lord will reward everyone for whatever good he does.

EPHESIANS 6:7–8

Jesus said to his host, "When you give a luncheon or dinner, do not invite your friends, your brothers or relatives, or your rich neighbors; if you do, they may invite you back and so you will be repaid. But when you give a banquet, invite the poor, the crippled, the lame, the blind, and you will be blessed. Although they cannot repay you, you will be repaid at the resurrection of the righteous."

LUKE 14:12–14

God ... reconciled us to himself through Christ and gave us the ministry of reconciliation.

2 CORINTHIANS 5:18

God was reconciling the world to himself in Christ, not counting men's sins against them. And he has committed to us the message of reconciliation. We are therefore Christ's ambassadors, as though God were making his appeal through us.

2 CORINTHIANS 5:19–20

Such confidence as this is ours through Christ before God. Not that we are competent in ourselves to claim anything for ourselves, but our competence comes from God. He has made us competent as ministers of a new covenant—not of the letter but of the Spirit; for the letter kills, but the Spirit gives life.

2 CORINTHIANS 3:4–6

NATURE

You alone are the LORD. You made the heavens, even the highest heavens, and all their starry host, the earth and all that is on it, the seas and all that is in them. You give life to everything, and the multitudes of heaven worship you.

NEHEMIAH 9:6

Since the creation of the world God's invisible qualities—his eternal power and divine nature—have been clearly seen, being understood from what has been made.

ROMANS 1:20

The LORD will indeed give what is good, and our land will yield its harvest.

PSALM 85:12

In the beginning you laid the foundations of the earth, and the heavens are the work of your hands.

PSALM 102:25

The heavens declare the glory of God; the skies proclaim the work of his hands.

PSALM 19:1

The LORD said,
  "As long as the earth endures,
  seedtime and harvest, . . .
  will never cease."

GENESIS 8:22

God said, "I give you every seed-bearing plant on
the face of the whole earth and every tree that has
fruit with seed in it. They will be yours for food.
And to all the beasts of the earth and all the birds of
the air and all the creatures that move on the
ground—everything that has the breath of life in it—
I give every green plant for food." And it was so.

GENESIS 1:29–30

By the word of the LORD were the heavens made,
  their starry host by the breath of his mouth.

PSALM 33:6

[Christ] is the image of the invisible God, the firstborn over all creation. For by him all things were
created: things in heaven and on earth, visible and
invisible, whether thrones or powers or rulers or
authorities; all things were created by him and
for him.

COLOSSIANS 1:15–16

199

OBEDIENCE

Jesus said, "If you obey my commands, you will remain in my love, just as I have obeyed my Father's commands and remain in his love. I have told you this so that my joy may be in you and that your joy may be complete."

JOHN 15:10–11

Jesus replied, "Blessed rather are those who hear the word of God and obey it."

LUKE 11:28

It is the LORD your God you must follow, and him you must revere. Keep his commands and obey him; serve him and hold fast to him.

DEUTERONOMY 13:4

If anyone obeys his word, God's love is truly made complete in him. This is how we know we are in him.

1 JOHN 2:5

If they obey and serve him,
  they will spend the rest of their days in prosperity
  and their years in contentment.

JOB 36:11

It is not those who hear the law who are righteous in God's sight, but it is those who obey the law who will be declared righteous.

ROMANS 2:13

I command you today to love the LORD your God, to walk in his ways, and to keep his commands, decrees and laws; then you will live and increase, and the LORD your God will bless you in the land you are entering to possess.

DEUTERONOMY 30:16

Jesus said, "Everyone who hears these words of mine and puts them into practice is like a wise man who built his house on the rock. The rain came down, the streams rose, and the winds blew and beat against that house; yet it did not fall, because it had its foundation on the rock."

MATTHEW 7:24–25

If you fully obey the LORD your God and carefully follow all his commands I give you today, the LORD your God will set you high above all the nations on earth.

DEUTERONOMY 28:1

PATIENCE

Be joyful in hope, patient in affliction,
faithful in prayer.

ROMANS 12:12

*Be patient, then, brothers, until the Lord's coming.
See how the farmer waits for the land to yield its
valuable crop and how patient he is for the autumn
and spring rains. You too, be patient and stand firm,
because the Lord's coming is near.*

JAMES 5:7–8

*If we hope for what we do not yet have, we wait
for it patiently.*

ROMANS 8:25

The end of a matter is better than
its beginning,
and patience is better than pride.

ECCLESIASTES 7:8

*I was shown mercy so that in me, the worst of sin-
ners, Christ Jesus might display his unlimited
patience as an example for those who would believe
on him and receive eternal life.*

1 TIMOTHY 1:16

We pray this in order that you may live a life worthy of the Lord and may please him in every way: bearing fruit in every good work, growing in the knowledge of God, being strengthened with all power according to his glorious might so that you may have great endurance and patience.

COLOSSIANS 1:10–11

A patient man has great understanding.

PROVERBS 14:29

The Lord is not slow in keeping his promise, as some understand slowness. He is patient with you, not wanting anyone to perish, but everyone to come to repentance.

2 PETER 3:9

*Through patience a ruler can be persuaded,
and a gentle tongue can break a bone.*

PROVERBS 25:15

PEACE

Glory, honor and peace for everyone
who does good: first for the Jew,
then for the Gentile. For God does
not show favoritism.

ROMANS 2:10–11

Great peace have they who love your law,
  and nothing can make them stumble.

PSALM 119:165

Peacemakers who sow in peace raise a harvest
of righteousness.

JAMES 3:18

You will keep in perfect peace
  him whose mind is steadfast,
  because he trust in you.

ISAIAH 26:3

When a man's ways are pleasing to the LORD,
  he makes even his enemies live at peace
    with him.

PROVERBS 16:7

The LORD blesses his people with peace.

PSALM 29:11

Since we have been justified through faith, we have peace with God through our Lord Jesus Christ.

ROMANS 5:1

Aim for perfection, listen to my appeal, be of one mind, live in peace. And the God of love and peace will be with you.

2 CORINTHIANS 13:11

I will listen to what God the LORD will say;
he promises peace to his people, his saints.

PSALM 85:8

The mind controlled by the Spirit is life and peace.

ROMANS 8:6

Consider the blameless, observe the upright;
there is a future for the man of peace.

PSALM 37:37

Jesus said,
"Blessed are the peacemakers,
for they will be called sons
of God."

MATTHEW 5:9

[Christ] himself is our peace, who has made the two
one and has destroyed the barrier, the dividing wall
of hostility.

EPHESIANS 2:14

Jesus said, "Peace I leave with you;
my peace I give you. I do not give
to you as the world gives. Do not
let your hearts be troubled and do
not be afraid."

JOHN 14:27

Grace and peace be yours in abundance through the knowledge of God and of Jesus our Lord.

2 PETER 1:2

The kingdom of God is not a matter of eating and drinking, but of righteousness, peace and joy in the Holy Spirit, because anyone who serves Christ in this way is pleasing to God and approved by men. Let us therefore make every effort to do what leads to peace and to mutual edification.

ROMANS 14:17–19

Let the peace of Christ rule in your hearts, since as members of one body you were called to peace.

COLOSSIANS 3:15

The God of peace will soon crush Satan under your feet.

ROMANS 16:20

PERSEVERANCE

The testing of your faith develops perseverance. Perseverance must finish its work so that you may be mature and complete, not lacking anything.

JAMES 1:3–4

To those who by persistence in doing good seek glory, honor and immortality, he will give eternal life.

ROMANS 2:7

Watch your life and doctrine closely. Persevere in them, because if you do, you will save both yourself and your hearers.

1 TIMOTHY 4:16

The God of all grace, who called you to his eternal glory in Christ, after you have suffered a little while, will himself restore you and make you strong, firm and steadfast.

1 PETER 5:10

You need to persevere so that when you have done the will of God, you will receive what he has promised.

HEBREWS 10:36

We consider blessed those who have persevered. You have heard of Job's perseverance and have seen what the Lord finally brought about. The Lord is full of compassion and mercy.

JAMES 5:11

Blessed is the man who perseveres under trial, because when he has stood the test, he will receive the crown of life that God has promised to those who love him.

JAMES 1:12

Let us not become weary in doing good, for at the proper time we will reap a harvest if we do not give up.

GALATIANS 6:9

Not that I have already obtained all this, or have already been made perfect, but I press on to take hold of that for which Christ Jesus took hold of me.

PHILIPPIANS 3:12

We also rejoice in our sufferings, because we know that suffering produces perseverance; perseverance, character; and character, hope.

ROMANS 5:3—4

POSSESSIONS

When God gives any man wealth and possessions, and enables him to enjoy them, to accept his lot and be happy in his work—this is a gift of God.

ECCLESIASTES 5:19

Jesus said, "Watch out! Be on your guard against all kinds of greed; a man's life does not consist in the abundance of his possessions."

LUKE 12:15

Delight yourself in the LORD
and he will give you the desires
of your heart.

PSALM 37:4

You sympathized with those in prison and joyfully accepted the confiscation of your property, because you knew that you yourselves had better and lasting possessions.

HEBREWS 10:34

*The LORD said,
"Ask of me,
and I will make the nations your inheritance,
the ends of the earth your possession."*

PSALM 2:8

If I give all I possess to the poor and surrender my body to the flames, but have not love, I gain nothing.

1 CORINTHIANS 13:3

Jesus said, "Seek first his kingdom and his righteousness, and all these things will be given to you as well."

MATTHEW 6:33

As servants of God we commend ourselves in every way: . . . poor, yet making many rich; having nothing, and yet possessing everything.

2 CORINTHIANS 6:4, 10

Jesus answered, "If you want to be perfect, go, sell your possessions and give to the poor, and you will have treasure in heaven. Then come, follow me."

MATTHEW 19:21

Jesus said, "Do not store up for yourselves treasures on earth, where moth and rust destroy, and where thieves break in and steal. But store up for yourselves treasures in heaven, where moth and rust do not destroy, and where thieves do not break in and steal. For where your treasure is, there your heart will be also."

MATTHEW 6:19–21

211

POWER

The God of Israel gives power and strength to his people.

PSALM 68:35

His divine power has given us everything we need for life and godliness through our knowledge of him who called us by his own glory and goodness.

2 PETER 1:3

By his power God raised the Lord from the dead, and he will raise us also.

1 CORINTHIANS 6:14

The LORD says, "I have raised you up for this very purpose, that I might show you my power and that my name might be proclaimed in all the earth."

EXODUS 9:16

The voice of the LORD is powerful.

PSALM 29:4

Wisdom makes one wise man more powerful than ten rulers in a city.

ECCLESIASTES 7:19

*[The Lord] said to me, "My grace is sufficient for
you, for my power is made perfect in weakness."
Therefore I will boast all the more gladly about my
weaknesses, so that Christ's power may rest on me.*

2 CORINTHIANS 12:9

I am the LORD, the God of all mankind. Is anything too hard for me?

JEREMIAH 32:27

*He gives strength to the weary
    and increases the power of the weak.*

ISAIAH 40:29

*God did not give us a spirit of timidity, but a spirit
of power.*

2 TIMOTHY 1:7

I am not ashamed of the gospel, because it is the power of God for the salvation of everyone who believes.

ROMANS 1:16

PRAISE & WORSHIP

*The trumpeters and singers joined in unison, as with
one voice, to give praise and thanks to the L*ORD*.
Accompanied by trumpets, cymbals and other
instruments, they raised their voices in praise to the
L*ORD *and sang:*
"He is good;
his love endures forever."
*Then the temple of the L*ORD *was filled with a
cloud, and the priests could not perform their service because of the cloud, for the glory of the L*ORD
filled the temple of God.

2 CHRONICLES 5:13–14

Come, let us bow down in worship,
*let us kneel before the L*ORD *our Maker.*

PSALM 95:6

Let everything that has breath praise the LORD.

PSALM 150:6

*I urge you, brothers, in view of God's mercy, to
offer your bodies as living sacrifices, holy and pleasing to God—this is your spiritual act of worship.*

ROMANS 12:1

I will praise you, O Lord my God, with all my heart;
    I will glorify your name forever.
For great is your love toward me;
    you have delivered me from the depths of the grave.

PSALM 86:12–13

The heavens praise your wonders, O Lord, your faithfulness too, in the assembly of the holy ones.

PSALM 89:5

Whenever the living creatures give glory, honor and thanks to him who sits on the throne and who lives for ever and ever, the twenty-four elders fall down before him who sits on the throne, and worship him who lives for ever and ever. They lay their crowns before the throne and say:
"You are worthy, our Lord and God,
    to receive glory and honor and power,
for you created all things,
    and by your will they were created
    and have their being."

REVELATION 4:9–11   **215**

PRAYER

"If my people, who are called by my name, will humble themselves and pray and seek my face and turn from their wicked ways, then will I hear from heaven and will forgive their sin and will heal their land," declares the LORD.

2 CHRONICLES 7:14

Jesus said, "When you stand praying, if you hold anything against anyone, forgive him, so that your Father in heaven may forgive you your sins."

MARK 11:25

"You will call upon me and come and pray to me, and I will listen to you," says the LORD. "You will seek me and find me when you seek me with all your heart."

JEREMIAH 29:12–13

The prayer of a righteous man is powerful and effective.

JAMES 5:16

Jesus said, "When you pray, go into your room, close the door and pray to your Father, who is unseen. Then your Father, who sees what is done in secret, will reward you."

MATTHEW 6:6

The LORD is far from the wicked but he hears the prayer of the righteous.

PROVERBS 15:29

The prayer offered in faith will make the sick person well; the Lord will raise him up. If he has sinned, he will be forgiven.

JAMES 5:15

*Let everyone who is godly pray to you
    while you may be found;
surely when the mighty waters rise,
    they will not reach him.*

PSALM 32:6

We have not stopped praying for you and asking God to fill you with the knowledge of his will through all spiritual wisdom and understanding.

COLOSSIANS 1:9

*The eyes of the Lord are on the righteous
    and his ears are attentive to their prayer.*

1 PETER 3:12

What other nation is so great as to have their gods near them the way the LORD our God is near us whenever we pray to him?

DEUTERONOMY 4:7

Jesus said, "If you remain in me and my words remain in you, ask whatever you wish, and it will be given you."

JOHN 15:7

I call to God,
    and the LORD saves me.
Evening, morning and noon
    I cry out in distress,
and he hears my voice.

PSALM 55:16–17

Do not be anxious about anything, but in every-thing, by prayer and petition, with thanksgiving, present your requests to God. And the peace of God, which transcends all understanding, will guard your hearts and your minds in Christ Jesus.

PHILIPPIANS 4:6–7

God has surely listened
   and heard my voice in prayer.
Praise be to God,
   who has not rejected my prayer
   or withheld his love from me!

PSALM 66:19–20

"Before they call I will answer;
   while they are still speaking I will hear,"
      says the LORD.

ISAIAH 65:24

Jesus said, "I tell you the truth, my Father will give
you whatever you ask in my name. Until now you
have not asked for anything in my name. Ask and
you will receive, and your joy will be complete."

JOHN 16:23–24

The Spirit helps us in our weakness. We do not
know what we ought to pray for, but he Spirit
himself intercedes for us with groans that words
cannot express.

ROMANS 8:26

PRIORITIES

O God, you are my God,
   earnestly I seek you;
my soul thirsts for you,
   my body longs for you,
in a dry and weary land
   where there is no water.

PSALM 63:1

*Look to the LORD and his strength;
   seek his face always.
Remember the wonders he has done,
   his miracles, and the judgments he pronounced.*

1 CHRONICLES 16:11–12

*Imitate those who through faith and patience inherit
what has been promised.*

HEBREWS 6:12

We fix our eyes not on what is seen,
but on what is unseen. For what is
seen is temporary, but what is
unseen is eternal.

2 CORINTHIANS 4:18

Jesus said, "If anyone would come after me, he must deny himself and take up his cross and follow me. For whoever wants to save his life will lose it, but whoever loses his life for me will find it."

MATTHEW 16:24–25

He who pursues righteousness and love
finds life, prosperity and honor.

PROVERBS 21:21

Let us fix our eyes on Jesus, the author and perfecter of our faith, who for the joy set before him endured the cross, scorning its shame, and sat down at the right hand of the throne of God.

HEBREWS 12:2

Jesus said, "Do not worry, saying, 'What shall we eat?' or 'What shall we drink?' or 'What shall we wear?' ... Seek first [God's] kingdom and his righteousness, and all these things will be given to you as well."

MATTHEW 6:31, 33

PROTECTION

If you make the Most High your dwelling—
even the LORD, who is my refuge—
then no harm will befall you,
no disaster will come near your tent.
For he will command his angels concerning you
to guard you in all your ways.

PSALM 91:9–11

The LORD watches over all who love him.

PSALM 145:20

The LORD will keep you from all harm—
he will watch over your life;
the LORD will watch over your coming and going
both now and forevermore.

PSALM 121:7–8

"No weapon forged against you will prevail,
and you will refute every tongue that
accuses you.
This is the heritage of the servants of the LORD,
and this is their vindication from me,"
declares the LORD.

ISAIAH 54:17

The Lord is faithful, and he will strengthen and protect you from the evil one.

2 THESSALONIANS 3:3

"Because he loves me," says the LORD, "I will
rescue him;
I will protect him, for he acknowledges my name.
He will call upon me, and I will answer him;
I will be with him in trouble,
I will deliver him and honor him."

PSALM 91:14–15

The LORD loves the just
and will not forsake his faithful
ones.
They will be protected forever.

PSALM 37:28

The eternal God is your refuge,
and underneath are the everlasting arms.

DEUTERONOMY 33:27

PROVISION

*God is able to make all grace abound to you, so
that in all things at all times, having all that you
need, you will abound in every good work.*

2 CORINTHIANS 9:8

> *Both high and low among men
> find refuge in the shadow of your wings.
> They feast on the abundance of your house;
> you give them drink from your river of delights.*

PSALM 36:7–8

Jesus said, "Your Father knows what you need before you ask him."

MATTHEW 6:8

*Jesus said, "If that is how God clothes the grass of
the field, which is here today and tomorrow is
thrown into the fire, will he not much more clothe
you, O you of little faith? So do not worry, saying,
'What shall we eat?' or 'What shall we drink?' or
'What shall we wear?' For the pagans run after all
these things, and your heavenly Father knows that
you need them."*

MATTHEW 6:30–32

My God will meet all your needs
according to his glorious riches in
Christ Jesus.

PHILIPPIANS 4:19

[God] has shown kindness by giving you rain from
heaven and crops in their seasons; he provides you
with plenty of food and fills your hearts with joy.

ACTS 14:17

Command those who are rich in this present
world not to be arrogant nor to put their hope in
wealth, which is so uncertain, but to put their
hope in God, who richly provides us with every-
thing for our enjoyment.

I TIMOTHY 6:17

The LORD will guide you always;
*   he will satisfy your needs in a sun-scorched land*
*   and will strengthen your frame.*
You will be like a well-watered garden,
*   like a spring whose waters never fail.*

ISAIAH 58:11

PURITY

How can a young man keep his way pure?
  By living according to your word.
I have hidden your word in my heart
  that I might not sin against you.

PSALM 119:9, 11

The wisdom that comes from heaven is first of all pure; then peace-loving, considerate, submissive, full of mercy and good fruit, impartial and sincere.

JAMES 3:17

If we walk in the light, as he is in the light, we have fellowship with one another, and the blood of Jesus, his Son, purifies us from all sin.

1 JOHN 1:7

He who loves a pure heart and whose speech is gracious will have the king for his friend.

PROVERBS 22:11

Don't let anyone look down on you because you are young, but set an example for the believers in speech, in life, in love, in faith and in purity.

1 TIMOTHY 4:12

Come near to God and he will come near to you.
Wash your hands, you sinners, and purify your
hearts, you double-minded. Grieve, mourn and wail.
Change your laughter to mourning and your joy to
gloom. Humble yourselves before the Lord, and he
will lift you up.

JAMES 4:8–10

Jesus said,
"Blessed are the pure in heart,
for they will see God."

MATTHEW 5:8

To the pure, all things are pure, but to those who
are corrupted and do not believe, nothing is pure.

TITUS 1:15

LORD, who may dwell in your sanctuary?
*   Who may live on your holy hill?*
He whose walk is blameless
*   and who does what is righteous,*
*   who speaks the truth from his heart.*

PSALM 15:1–2

PURPOSE

I cry out to God Most High,
   to God, who fulfills his purpose
      for me.

PSALM 57:2

We know that in all things God works for the good of those who love him, who have been called according to his purpose.

ROMANS 8:28

We are God's workmanship, created in Christ Jesus to do good works, which God prepared in advance for us to do.

EPHESIANS 2:10

*The plans of the LORD stand firm forever,
   the purposes of his heart through all
      generations.*

PSALM 33:11

Everyone who confesses the name of the Lord must turn away from wickedness. If a man cleanses himself . . . he will be an instrument for noble purposes, made holy, useful to the Master and prepared to do any good work.

2 TIMOTHY 2:19, 21

The LORD will fulfill his purpose for me;
your love, O LORD, endures forever—
do not abandon the works of your hands.

PSALM 138:8

We constantly pray for you, that our God may
count you worthy of his calling, and that by his
power he may fulfill every good purpose of yours
and every act prompted by your faith.

2 THESSALONIANS 1:11

Many are the plans in a man's heart, but it is the LORD's purpose that prevails.

PROVERBS 19:21

Because God wanted to make the unchanging
nature of his purpose very clear to the heirs of what
was promised, he confirmed it with an oath.

HEBREWS 6:17

The LORD Almighty has sworn,
"Surely, as I have planned, so it will be,
and as I have purposed, so it will stand."

ISAIAH 14:24

QUIETNESS
& SOLITUDE

Make it your ambition to lead a quiet life, to mind your own business and to work with your hands.

I THESSALONIANS 4:11

The fruit of righteousness will be peace;
    the effect of righteousness will be quietness
        and confidence forever.

ISAIAH 32:17

Be still, and know that I am God;
    I will be exalted among the nations,
    I will be exalted in the earth.

PSALM 46:10

I urge, then, first of all, that requests, prayers, intercession and thanksgiving be made for everyone—for kings and all those in authority, that we may live peaceful and quiet lives in all godliness and holiness. This is good, and pleases God our Savior, who wants all men to be saved and to come to a knowledge of the truth.

I TIMOTHY 2:1–4

Better a dry crust with peace and quiet
   than a house full of feasting, with strife.

PROVERBS 17:1

I say to myself, "The LORD is my portion;
   therefore I will wait for him."
The LORD is good to those whose hope is in him,
   to the one who seeks him;
it is good to wait quietly
   for the salvation of the LORD.

LAMENTATIONS 3:24–26

I have stilled and quieted my soul;
   like a weaned child with its mother,
   like a weaned child is my soul within me.

PSALM 131:2

The LORD will fight for you; you need only to be still.

EXODUS 14:14

REDEMPTION

*All have sinned and fall short of the glory of God,
and are justified freely by his grace through the
redemption that came by Christ Jesus.*

ROMANS 3:23–24

*We ourselves, who have the firstfruits of the Spirit,
groan inwardly as we wait eagerly for our adoption
as sons, the redemption of our bodies.*

ROMANS 8:23

*In [Christ] we have redemption through his blood,
the forgiveness of sins, in accordance with the riches
of God's grace that he lavished on us with all wisdom
and understanding.*

EPHESIANS 1:7–8

Put your hope in the LORD,
for with the LORD is unfailing love
and with him is full redemption.

PSALM 130:7

*[God] has rescued us from the dominion of darkness
and brought us into the kingdom of the Son he loves,
in whom we have redemption, the forgiveness of sins.*

COLOSSIANS 1:13–14

[God] redeemed us in order that the blessing given to Abraham might come to the Gentiles through Christ Jesus.

GALATIANS 3:14

It was not with perishable things such as silver or gold that you were redeemed from the empty way of life handed down to you from your forefathers, but with the precious blood of Christ, a lamb without blemish or defect.

1 PETER 1:18–19

The LORD says,
"I have swept away your offenses like a cloud,
    your sins like the morning mist.
Return to me,
    for I have redeemed you."

ISAIAH 44:22

Praise the LORD. . . .
He provided redemption for his people;
    he ordained his covenant forever—
    holy and awesome is his name.

PSALM 111:1, 9

REJECTION

Do not hide your face from me,
do not turn your servant away in anger;
you have been my helper.
Do not reject me or forsake me,
O God my Savior.
Though my father and mother forsake me,
the LORD will receive me.

PSALM 27:9–10

Jesus said, "All that the Father gives me will come
to me, and whoever comes to me I will never drive
away. For I have come down from heaven not to do
my will but to do the will of him who sent me. And
this is the will of him who sent me, that I shall lose
none of all that he has given me, but raise them up
at the last day."

JOHN 6:37–39

Jesus said, "He who listens to you listens to me; he who rejects you rejects me; but he who rejects me rejects him who sent me."

LUKE 10:16

The LORD will not reject his people;
he will never forsake his inheritance.

PSALM 94:14

For the sake of his great name the
LORD will not reject his people,
because the LORD was pleased to
make you his own.

I SAMUEL 12:22

Those who know your name will trust in you,
for you, LORD, have never forsaken those who
seek you.

PSALM 9:10

Looking at his disciples, [Jesus] said:
"Blessed are you when men hate you,
when they exclude you and insult you
and reject your name as evil, because of the
Son of Man."

LUKE 6:20, 22

RELATIONSHIPS

Carry each other's burdens, and in this way you will fulfill the law of Christ.

GALATIANS 6:2

*A man of many companions may come to ruin,
    but there is a friend who sticks closer than
        a brother.*

PROVERBS 18:24

*Be devoted to one another in brotherly love. Honor
one another above yourselves.*

ROMANS 12:10

*Jesus said, "A new command I give you: Love one
another. As I have loved you, so you must love one
another. By this all men will know that you are my
disciples, if you love one another."*

JOHN 13:34–35

He who walks with the wise grows wise.

PROVERBS 13:20

*Jesus said, "I tell you the truth, whatever you did
for one of the least of these brothers of mine, you
did for me."*

MATTHEW 25:40

Jesus said, "Here I am! I stand at the door and knock. If anyone hears my voice and opens the door, I will come in and eat with him, and he with me."

REVELATION 3:20

Jesus said, "My command is this: Love each other as I have loved you. Greater love has no one than this, that he lay down his life for his friends."

JOHN 15:12–13

Two are better than one,
    because they have a good return for their work:
If one falls down,
    his friend can help him up.
But pity the man who falls
    and has no one to help him up!
Also, if two lie down together, they will keep warm.
    But how can one keep warm alone?
Though one may be overpowered,
    two can defend themselves.
A cord of three strands is not quickly broken.

ECCLESIASTES 4:9–12

RENEWAL

The LORD says, "I will give you a new heart and put a new spirit in you; I will remove from you your heart of stone and give you a heart of flesh. And I will put my Spirit in you and move you to follow my decrees and be careful to keep my laws."

EZEKIEL 36:26–27

Create in me a pure heart, O God,
and renew a steadfast spirit within me.

PSALM 51:10

Though outwardly we are wasting away, yet inwardly we are being renewed day by day.

2 CORINTHIANS 4:16

Be made new in the attitude of your minds.

EPHESIANS 4:23

Don't you know that all of us who were baptized into Christ Jesus were baptized into his death? We were therefore buried with him through baptism into death in order that, just as Christ was raised from the dead through the glory of the Father, we too may live a new life.

ROMANS 6:3–4

See, I am doing a new thing!
    Now it springs up; do you not perceive it?
I am making a way in the desert
    and streams in the wasteland.

ISAIAH 43:19

You have taken off your old self with its practices
and have put on the new self, which is being
renewed in knowledge in the image of its Creator.

COLOSSIANS 3:9–10

We eagerly await a Savior from [heaven], the Lord
Jesus Christ, who, by the power that enables him
to bring everything under his control, will trans-
form our lowly bodies so that they will be like his
glorious body.

PHILIPPIANS 3:20–21

This is what the Sovereign LORD says:
"Behold, I will create
    new heavens and a new earth.
The former things will not be
        remembered,
    nor will they come to mind."

ISAIAH 65:17

REPENTANCE

Jesus said, "I tell you that . . . there will be more rejoicing in heaven over one sinner who repents than over ninety-nine righteous persons who do not need to repent."

LUKE 15:7

Repent, then, and turn to God, so that your sins may be wiped out, that times of refreshing may come from the Lord.

ACTS 3:19

The Lord is not slow in keeping his promise, as some understand slowness. He is patient with you, not wanting anyone to perish, but everyone to come to repentance.

2 PETER 3:9

Jesus answered them, "It is not the healthy who need a doctor, but the sick. I have not come to call the righteous, but sinners to repentance."

LUKE 5:31–32

Godly sorrow brings repentance that leads to salvation and leaves no regret.

2 CORINTHIANS 7:10

Peter replied, "Repent and be baptized, every one of you, in the name of Jesus Christ for the forgiveness of your sins. And you will receive the gift of the Holy Spirit."

ACTS 2:38

The LORD said:
"If my people, who are called by my name, will humble themselves and pray and seek my face and turn from their wicked ways, then will I hear from heaven and will forgive their sin and will heal their land."

2 CHRONICLES 7:14

This is what the Sovereign LORD, the Holy One
          of Israel, says:
"In repentance and rest is your salvation,
     in quietness and trust is your strength."

ISAIAH 30:15

Let the wicked forsake his way
     and the evil man his thoughts.
Let him turn to the LORD, and he will have mercy
          on him,
     and to our God, for he will freely pardon.

ISAIAH 55:7

If a wicked man turns away from all the sins he has committed and keeps all my decrees and does what is just and right, he will surely live; he will not die. None of the offenses he has committed will be remembered against him. Because of the righteous things he has done, he will live.

EZEKIEL 18:21–22

This is what the LORD says:
"If you repent, I will restore you
that you may serve me."

JEREMIAH 15:19

Jesus said, "These are the words of the Amen, the faithful and true witness, the ruler of God's creation. . . . Those whom I love I rebuke and discipline. So be earnest, and repent."

REVELATION 3:14, 19

Jesus said, "If your brother sins, rebuke him, and if he repents, forgive him. If he sins against you seven times in a day, and seven times comes back to you and says, 'I repent,' forgive him."

LUKE 17:3–4

Whenever anyone turns to the Lord, the veil is taken away. Now the Lord is the Spirit, and where the Spirit of the Lord is, there is freedom.

2 CORINTHIANS 3:16–17

*He who conceals his sins does not prosper,
    but whoever confesses and renounces them
        finds mercy.*

PROVERBS 28:13

*"The Redeemer will come to Zion,
    to those in Jacob who repent of their sins,"
declares the LORD.*

ISAIAH 59:20

Jesus said, "I tell you, there is rejoicing in the presence of the angels of God over one sinner who repents."

LUKE 15:10

REST

Jesus said, "Come to me, all you who are weary and burdened, and I will give you rest. Take my yoke upon you and learn from me, for I am gentle and humble in heart, and you will find rest for your souls. For my yoke is easy and my burden is light."

MATTHEW 11:28–30

There remains, then, a Sabbath-rest for the people of God; for anyone who enters God's rest also rests from his own work, just as God did from his. Let us, therefore, make every effort to enter that rest.

HEBREWS 4:9–11

This is what the LORD Almighty says: "I will refresh the weary and satisfy the faint."

JEREMIAH 31:25

My soul finds rest in God alone;
*   my salvation comes from him.*
He alone is my rock and my salvation;
*   he is my fortress, I will never be shaken.*

PSALM 62:1–2

Be at rest once more, O my soul,
 for the Lord has been good
  to you.

Psalm 116:7

He who dwells in the shelter of the Most High
 will rest in the shadow of the Almighty.

Psalm 91:1

My people will live in peaceful dwelling places,
 in secure homes,
 in undisturbed places of rest.

Isaiah 32:18

The Lord is my shepherd, I shall not be in want.
 He makes me lie down in green pastures,
he leads me beside quiet waters,
 he restores my soul.
He guides me in paths of righteousness
 for his name's sake.

Psalm 23:1–3

RESTORATION

The LORD says, "I will search for the lost and bring back the strays. I will bind up the injured and strengthen the weak."

EZEKIEL 34:16

When you and your children return to the LORD your God and obey him with all your heart and with all your soul according to everything I command you today, then the LORD your God will restore your fortunes and have compassion on you.

DEUTERONOMY 30:2–3

"I will restore you to health and heal your wounds," declares the LORD.

JEREMIAH 30:17

Though you have made me see troubles, many and bitter,
*   you will restore my life again;*
from the depths of the earth
*   you will again bring me up.*
You will increase my honor
*   and comfort me once again.*

PSALM 71:20–21

The LORD says,
"I will repay you for the years the locusts have
          eaten—
     the great locust and the young locust,
     the other locusts and the locust swarm—
my great army that I sent among you.
You will have plenty to eat, until you are full,
     and you will praise the name of the LORD
          your God,
     who has worked wonders for you;
never again will my people be shamed."

JOEL 2:25–26

The God of all grace, who called you to his eternal
glory in Christ, after you have suffered a little while,
will himself restore you and make you strong, firm
and steadfast.

1 PETER 5:10

Restore us, O God;
make your face shine upon us,
that we may be saved.

PSALM 80:3

REWARD

Whatever you do, work at it with all your heart, as working for the Lord, not for men, since you know that you will receive an inheritance from the Lord as a reward. It is the Lord Christ you are serving.

COLOSSIANS 3:23–24

You know that the Lord will reward everyone for whatever good he does.

EPHESIANS 6:8

Jesus said, "Behold, I am coming soon! My reward is with me, and I will give to everyone according to what he has done."

REVELATION 22:12

Jesus said, "When you pray, go into your room, close the door and pray to your Father, who is unseen. Then your Father, who sees what is done in secret, will reward you."

MATTHEW 6:6

Jesus said, "If anyone gives even a cup of cold water to one of these little ones because he is my disciple, I tell you the truth, he will certainly not lose his reward."

MATTHEW 10:42

Jesus said, "Blessed are you when people insult you, persecute you and falsely say all kinds of evil against you because of me. Rejoice and be glad, because great is your reward in heaven."

MATTHEW 5:11–12

*I the LORD search the heart
    and examine the mind,
to reward a man according to his conduct,
    according to what his deeds deserve.*

JEREMIAH 17:10

Fire will test the quality of each man's work. If what he has built survives, he will receive his reward.

1 CORINTHIANS 3:13–14

Jesus said, "Love your enemies, do good to them, and lend to them without expecting to get anything back. Then your reward will be great, and you will be sons of the Most High."

LUKE 6:35

RIGHTEOUSNESS

The fruit of the righteous is a tree of life,
and he who wins souls is wise.

PROVERBS 11:30

The path of the righteous is like the first gleam
of dawn,
shining ever brighter till the full light of day.

PROVERBS 4:18

Jesus said,
"Blessed are those who hunger and
thirst for righteousness,
for they will be filled."

MATTHEW 5:6

[God] does not take his eyes off the righteous;
he enthrones them with kings
and exalts them forever.

JOB 36:7

In the way of righteousness there
is life;
along that path is immortality.

PROVERBS 12:28

God made him who had no sin to be sin for us, so that in him we might become the righteousness of God.

2 CORINTHIANS 5:21

Do not let anyone lead you astray. He who does what is right is righteous, just as [God] is righteous.

1 JOHN 3:7

The eyes of the Lord are on the righteous and his ears are attentive to their prayer.

1 PETER 3:12

The righteous are as bold as a lion.

PROVERBS 28:1

The mouth of the righteous man utters wisdom, and his tongue speaks what is just. The law of his God is in his heart; his feet do not slip.

PSALM 37:30–31

SACRIFICE

I urge you, brothers, in view of God's mercy, to offer your bodies as living sacrifices, holy and pleasing to God—this is your spiritual act of worship.

ROMANS 12:1

Through Jesus ... let us continually offer to God a sacrifice of praise—the fruit of lips that confess his name. And do not forget to do good and to share with others, for with such sacrifices God is pleased.

HEBREWS 13:15–16

As you come to him, the living Stone—rejected by men but chosen by God and precious to him—you also, like living stones, are being built into a spiritual house to be a holy priesthood, offering spiritual sacrifices acceptable to God through Jesus Christ.

I PETER 2:4–5

Be silent before the Sovereign LORD,
    for the day of the LORD is near.
The LORD has prepared a sacrifice;
    he has consecrated those he has invited.

ZEPHANIAH 1:7

O LORD, *open my lips,*
and my mouth will declare your praise....
The sacrifices of God are a broken spirit;
a broken and contrite heart,
O God, you will not despise.

PSALM 51:15, 17

To do what is right and just
is more acceptable to the LORD
than sacrifice.

PROVERBS 21:3

I will sacrifice a freewill offering to you;
I will praise your name, O LORD,
for it is good.
For he has delivered me from all my troubles,
and my eyes have looked in triumph on my foes.

PSALM 54:6–7

SALVATION

*If you confess with your mouth, "Jesus is Lord,"
and believe in your heart that God raised him from
the dead, you will be saved. For it is with your heart
that you believe and are justified, and it is with your
mouth that you confess and are saved.*

ROMANS 10:9–10

*The hour has come for you to wake up from your
slumber, because our salvation is nearer now than
when we first believed. The night is nearly over; the
day is almost here. So let us put aside the deeds of
darkness and put on the armor of light.*

ROMANS 13:11–12

*Like newborn babies, crave pure spiritual milk, so
that by it you may grow up in your salvation, now
that you have tasted that the Lord is good.*

1 PETER 2:2–3

**Believe in the Lord Jesus, and you will
be saved—you and your household.**

ACTS 16:31

*Continue to work out your salvation with fear and
trembling, for it is God who works in you to will
and to act according to his good purpose.*

PHILIPPIANS 2:12–13

Once made perfect, [Jesus] became the source of eternal salvation for all who obey him.

HEBREWS 5:9

Now is the time of God's favor, now is the day of salvation.

2 CORINTHIANS 6:2

Christ was sacrificed once to take away the sins of many people; and he will appear a second time, not to bear sin, but to bring salvation to those who are waiting for him.

HEBREWS 9:28

The salvation of the righteous comes from
        the LORD;
    he is their stronghold in time of trouble.

PSALM 37:39

God did not appoint us to suffer wrath but to receive salvation through our Lord Jesus Christ. He died for us so that, whether we are awake or asleep, we may live together with him.

1 THESSALONIANS 5:9–10

SATISFACTION

You open your hand, O LORD,
   and satisfy the desires of every
      living thing.

PSALM 145:16

The LORD will guide you always;
   he will satisfy your needs in a sun-scorched land
   and will strengthen your frame.
You will be like a well-watered garden,
   like a spring whose waters never fail.

ISAIAH 58:11

With long life will I satisfy him
   and show him my salvation.

PSALM 91:16

A man can do nothing better than to eat and drink
and find satisfaction in his work. This too, I see, is
from the hand of God.

ECCLESIASTES 2:24

Jesus said,
"Blessed are you who hunger now,
   for you will be satisfied."

LUKE 6:21

My soul will be satisfied as with the richest of foods;
  with singing lips my mouth will praise you.

PSALM 63:5

The LORD declares,
"Come, all you who are thirsty,
come to the waters;
and you who have no money,
  come, buy and eat!
Come, buy wine and milk
  without money and without cost.
Why spend money on what is not bread,
  and your labor on what does not satisfy?
Listen, listen to me, and eat what is good,
  and your soul will delight in the richest of fare."

ISAIAH 55:1–2

[The LORD] satisfies your desires with good things so that your youth is renewed like the eagle's.

PSALM 103:5

SECURITY

A righteous man will be remembered forever.
He will have no fear of bad news;
  his heart is steadfast, trusting in the LORD.
His heart is secure, he will have no fear;
  in the end he will look in triumph on his foes.

PSALM 112:6–8

My people will live in peaceful dwelling places,
  in secure homes,
  in undisturbed places of rest.
Though hail flattens the forest
  and the city is leveled completely,
how blessed you will be.

ISAIAH 32:18–20

Do not take advantage of each other, but fear your God. I am the LORD your God. Follow my decrees and be careful to obey my laws, and you will live safely in the land. Then the land will yield its fruit, and you will eat your fill and live there in safety.

LEVITICUS 25:17–19

Let the beloved of the L ORD rest secure in him,
for he shields him all day long,
and the one the L ORD loves rests between
his shoulders.

DEUTERONOMY 33:12

I will lie down and sleep in peace,
for you alone, O L ORD,
make me dwell in safety.

PSALM 4:8

The name of the L ORD is a strong tower;
the righteous run to it and are safe.

PROVERBS 18:10

I have set the L ORD always before me.
Because he is at my right hand,
I will not be shaken.
Therefore my heart is glad and my tongue rejoices;
my body also will rest secure.

PSALM 16:8–9

SEEKING GOD

"*You will call upon me and come and pray to me,
and I will listen to you. You will seek me and find
me when you seek me with all your heart. I will be
found by you,*" *declares the* LORD.

JEREMIAH 29:12–14

Let the hearts of those who seek the LORD *rejoice.
Look to the* LORD *and his strength;*
seek his face always.

PSALM 105:3–4

Without faith it is impossible to
please God, because anyone who
comes to him must believe that he
exists and that he rewards those
who earnestly seek him.

HEBREWS 11:6

*If you will look to God
and plead with the Almighty,
if you are pure and upright,
even now he will rouse himself on your behalf
and restore you to your rightful place.*

JOB 8:5–6

Sow for yourselves righteousness,
    reap the fruit of unfailing love,
and break up your unplowed ground;
    for it is time to seek the LORD,
until he comes
    and showers righteousness on you.

HOSEA 10:12

Jesus said, "Ask and it will be given to you; seek
and you will find; knock and the door will be
opened to you. For everyone who asks receives; he
who seeks finds; and to him who knocks, the door
will be opened."

LUKE 11:9–10

Seek the LORD while he may be found;
    call on him while he is near.
Let the wicked forsake his way
    and the evil man his thoughts.
Let him turn to the LORD, and he will have mercy
        on him,
    and to our God, for he will freely pardon.

ISAIAH 55:6–7

SELF-CONTROL

Live self-controlled, upright and godly lives in this present age, while we wait for the blessed hope—the glorious appearing of our great God and Savior, Jesus Christ.

TITUS 2:12–13

The end of all things is near. Therefore be clear minded and self-controlled so that you can pray.

I PETER 4:7

Since we belong to the day, let us be self-controlled, putting on faith and love as a breastplate, and the hope of salvation as a helmet.

I THESSALONIANS 5:8

Prepare your minds for action; be self-controlled; set your hope fully on the grace to be given you when Jesus Christ is revealed.

I PETER 1:13

Since an overseer is entrusted with God's work, he must be blameless—not overbearing, not quick-tempered, not given to drunkenness, not violent. . . . Rather he must be . . . self-controlled, upright, holy and disciplined.

TITUS 1:7–8

Be self-controlled and alert. Your enemy the devil prowls around like a roaring lion looking for someone to devour. Resist him, standing firm in the faith.

1 PETER 5:8–9

No temptation has seized you except what is common to man. And God is faithful; he will not let you be tempted beyond what you can bear. But when you are tempted, he will also provide a way out so that you can stand up under it.

1 CORINTHIANS 10:13

If by the Spirit you put to death the misdeeds of the body, you will live, because those who are led by the Spirit of God are sons of God.

ROMANS 8:13–14

The fruit of the Spirit is . . . self-control.

GALATIANS 5:22–23

Be careful, and watch yourselves closely so that you do not forget the things your eyes have seen or let them slip from your heart as long as you live. Teach them to your children and to their children after them.

DEUTERONOMY 4:9

SELF-ESTEEM

[God] chose us in him before the creation of the world to be holy and blameless in his sight. In love he predestined us to be adopted as his sons through Jesus Christ, in accordance with his pleasure and will.

EPHESIANS 1:4–5

"I have engraved you on the palms of my hands;
    your walls are ever before me,"
    declares the LORD.

ISAIAH 49:16

Know that the LORD is God.
    It is he who made us, and we are his;
    we are his people, the sheep of his pasture.

PSALM 100:3

Do you not know that your body is a temple of the Holy Spirit, who is in you, whom you have received from God? You are not your own; you were bought at a price. Therefore honor God with your body.

1 CORINTHIANS 6:19–20

Don't you know that you yourselves are God's temple and that God's Spirit lives in you?

1 CORINTHIANS 3:16

The LORD says,
"You are precious and honored in my sight,
*   and ... I love you."*

ISAIAH 43:4

You have put on the new self, which is being renewed in knowledge in the image of its Creator.

COLOSSIANS 3:10

For you created my inmost being;
*   you knit me together in my mother's womb.*
I praise you because I am fearfully and wonderfully
*   made;*
*   your works are wonderful,*
*   I know that full well.*

PSALM 139:13–14

Jesus said, "Are not two sparrows sold for a penny?
Yet not one of them will fall to the ground apart
from the will of your Father. And even the very hairs
of your head are all numbered. So don't be afraid;
you are worth more than many sparrows."

MATTHEW 10:29–31

SERVICE

Serve wholeheartedly, as if you were serving the Lord, not men, because you know that the Lord will reward everyone for whatever good he does.

EPHESIANS 6:7–8

Though I am free and belong to no man, I make myself a slave to everyone, to win as many as possible. . . . I have become all things to all men so that by all possible means I might save some.

I CORINTHIANS 9:19, 22

Jesus said, "Whoever serves me must follow me; and where I am, my servant also will be. My Father will honor the one who serves me."

JOHN 12:26

There are different kinds of service, but the same Lord.

I CORINTHIANS 12:5

Acknowledge the God of your father, and serve him with wholehearted devotion and with a willing mind, for the LORD searches every heart and understands every motive behind the thoughts.

I CHRONICLES 28:9

I glory in Christ Jesus in my service to God.

ROMANS 15:17

I thank Christ Jesus our Lord, who has given me strength, that he considered me faithful, appointing me to his service.

1 TIMOTHY 1:12

Whatever you do, work at it with all your heart, as working for the Lord, not for men, since you know that you will receive an inheritance from the Lord as a reward. It is the Lord Christ you are serving.

COLOSSIANS 3:23–24

This service that you perform is not only supplying the needs of God's people but is also overflowing in many expressions of thanks to God. Because of the service by which you have proved yourselves, men will praise God for the obedience that accompanies your confession of the gospel of Christ, and for your generosity in sharing with them and with everyone else.

2 CORINTHIANS 9:12–13

SINCERITY

Love must be sincere. Hate what is evil; cling to what is good. Be devoted to one another in brotherly love. Honor one another above yourselves.

ROMANS 12:9–10

Now this is our boast: Our conscience testifies that we have conducted ourselves in the world, and especially in our relations with you, in the holiness and sincerity that are from God. We have done so not according to worldly wisdom but according to God's grace.

2 CORINTHIANS 1:12

My words come from an upright heart;
    my lips sincerely speak what I know.

JOB 33:3

For Christ, our Passover lamb, has been sacrificed. Therefore let us keep the Festival, not with the old yeast, the yeast of malice and wickedness, but with bread without yeast, the bread of sincerity and truth.

1 CORINTHIANS 5:7–8

Since we have a great priest over the house of God, let us draw near to God with a sincere heart in full assurance of faith, having our hearts sprinkled to cleanse us from a guilty conscience and having our bodies washed with pure water. Let us hold unswervingly to the hope we profess, for he who promised is faithful.

HEBREWS 10:21–23

The goal of this command is love, which comes from a pure heart and a good conscience and a sincere faith.

1 TIMOTHY 1:5

Unlike so many, we do not peddle the word of God for profit. On the contrary, in Christ we speak before God with sincerity, like men sent from God.

2 CORINTHIANS 2:17

Now that you have purified yourselves by obeying the truth so that you have sincere love for your brothers, love one another deeply, from the heart.

1 PETER 1:22

SPEECH

Whoever would love life and see good days must keep his tongue from evil and his lips from deceitful speech.

I PETER 3:10

The speech of the upright rescues them.

PROVERBS 12:6

He who loves a pure heart and whose speech
*   is gracious*
* will have the king for his friend.*

PROVERBS 22:11

In your teaching show integrity, seriousness and soundness of speech that cannot be condemned, so that those who oppose you may be ashamed because they have nothing bad to say about us.

TITUS 2:7–8

The quiet words of the wise are more to be heeded than the shouts of a ruler of fools.

ECCLESIASTES 9:17

He who guards his mouth and his tongue keeps himself from calamity.

PROVERBS 21:23

*Let your conversation be always full of grace,
seasoned with salt, so that you may know how to
answer everyone.*

COLOSSIANS 4:6

Pleasant words are a honeycomb, sweet to the soul and healing to the bones.

PROVERBS 16:24

*Moses said to the LORD, "O Lord, I have never
been eloquent, neither in the past nor since you have
spoken to your servant. I am slow of speech and
tongue." The LORD said to him, "Who gave man his
mouth? Who makes him deaf or mute? Who gives
him sight or makes him blind? Is it not I, the LORD?
Now go; I will help you speak and will teach you
what to say."*

EXODUS 4:10–12

*Jesus said, "Do not worry beforehand about what
to say. Just say whatever is given you at the time, for
it is not you speaking, but the Holy Spirit."*

MARK 13:11

SPIRITUAL GROWTH

Like newborn babies, crave pure spiritual milk, so that by it you may grow up in your salvation, now that you have tasted that the Lord is good.

1 PETER 2:2–3

We will no longer be infants, tossed back and forth by the waves, and blown here and there by every wind of teaching and by the cunning and craftiness of men in their deceitful scheming. Instead, speaking the truth in love, we will in all things grow up into him who is the Head, that is, Christ.

EPHESIANS 4:14–15

Keep your father's commands
*   and do not forsake your mother's teaching.*
For these commands are a lamp,
*   this teaching is a light,*
and the corrections of discipline
*   are the way to life.*

PROVERBS 6:20, 23

Do your best to present yourself to God as one approved, a workman who does not need to be ashamed and who correctly handles the word of truth.

2 TIMOTHY 2:15

Those who belong to Christ Jesus have crucified the sinful nature with its passions and desires. Since we live by the Spirit, let us keep in step with the Spirit.

GALATIANS 5:24–25

Jesus said, "I am the vine; you are the branches. If a man remains in me and I in him, he will bear much fruit; apart from me you can do nothing."

JOHN 15:5

Put on the full armor of God, so that when the day of evil comes, you may be able to stand your ground, and after you have done everything, to stand. Stand firm then, with the belt of truth buckled around your waist, with the breastplate of righteousness in place, and with your feet fitted with the readiness that comes from the gospel of peace. In addition to all this, take up the shield of faith, with which you can extinguish all the flaming arrows of the evil one. Take the helmet of salvation and the sword of the Spirit, which is the word of God.

EPHESIANS 6:13–17

STABILITY

I have set the LORD always before me.
Because he is at my right hand,
I will not be shaken.

PSALM 16:8

You, O LORD, have delivered my soul from death,
my eyes from tears,
my feet from stumbling,
that I may walk before the LORD
in the land of the living.

PSALM 116:8–9

My soul finds rest in God alone;
my salvation comes from him.
He alone is my rock and my salvation;
he is my fortress, I will never be shaken.

PSALM 62:1–2

The God of all grace, who called you to his eternal glory in Christ, after you have suffered a little while, will himself restore you and make you strong, firm and steadfast.

1 PETER 5:10

Great peace have they who love your law,
and nothing can make them stumble.

PSALM 119:165

If the LORD delights in a man's way,
he makes his steps firm;
though he stumble, he will not fall,
for the LORD upholds him with his hand.

PSALM 37:23–24

Whoever loves his brother lives in the light, and there is nothing in him to make him stumble.

I JOHN 2:10

To him who is able to keep you from falling and to
present you before his glorious presence without
fault and with great joy—to the only God our
Savior be glory, majesty, power and authority,
through Jesus Christ our Lord, before all ages, now
and forevermore! Amen.

JUDE vv.24–25

STEWARDSHIP

Men ought to regard us as servants of Christ and as those entrusted with the secret things of God. Now it is required that those who have been given a trust must prove faithful.

1 CORINTHIANS 4:1–2

Good will come to him who is
generous and lends freely,
who conducts his affairs with justice.

PSALM 112:5

Jesus said, "From everyone who has been given much, much will be demanded; and from the one who has been entrusted with much, much more will be asked."

LUKE 12:48

Since an overseer is entrusted with God's work, he must be blameless—not overbearing, not quick-tempered, not given to drunkenness, not violent, not pursuing dishonest gain. Rather he must be hospitable, one who loves what is good, who is self-controlled, upright, holy and disciplined. He must hold firmly to the trustworthy message as it has been taught, so that he can encourage others by sound doctrine and refute those who oppose it.

TITUS 1:7–9

Each one should use whatever gift he has received to serve others, faithfully administering God's grace in its various forms. If anyone speaks, he should do it as one speaking the very words of God. If anyone serves, he should do it with the strength God provides, so that in all things God may be praised through Jesus Christ.

1 PETER 4:10–11

Jesus said, "[The kingdom of heaven] will be like a man going on a journey, who called his servants and entrusted his property to them. To one he gave five talents of money, to another two talents, and to another one talent, each according to his ability. Then he went on his journey. The man who had received the five talents went at once and put his money to work and gained five more. . . . After a long time the master of those servants returned and settled accounts with them. The man who had received the five talents brought the other five. 'Master,' he said, 'you entrusted me with five talents. See, I have gained five more.' His master replied, 'Well done, good and faithful servant! You have been faithful with a few things; I will put you in charge of many things. Come and share your master's happiness!' "

MATTHEW 25:14–16, 19–21   277

STRENGTH

*You do not lack any spiritual gift as you eagerly
wait for our Lord Jesus Christ to be revealed. He
will keep you strong to the end.*

1 CORINTHIANS 1:7–8

I can do everything through [Christ]
who gives me strength.

PHILIPPIANS 4:13

*God is our refuge and strength,
    an ever-present help in trouble.*

PSALM 46:1

The LORD gives strength to his people.

PSALM 29:11

Those who hope in the LORD
    will renew their strength.
They will soar on wings like eagles;
    they will run and not grow weary,
    they will walk and not be faint.

ISAIAH 40:31

Do not fear, for I am with you;
do not be dismayed, for I am your God.
I will strengthen you and help you;
I will uphold you with my righteous right hand.

ISAIAH 41:10

My flesh and my heart may fail,
but God is the strength of my heart
and my portion forever.

PSALM 73:26

May [the Lord] strengthen your hearts so that you will be blameless and holy in the presence of our God and Father when our Lord Jesus comes with all his holy ones.

1 THESSALONIANS 3:13

O my Strength, I watch for you;
you, O God, are my fortress, my loving God.
God will go before me
and will let me gloat over those who slander me.

PSALM 59:9–10

The LORD is my strength and my shield;
  my heart trusts in him, and I am helped.

PSALM 28:7

I will sing of your strength,
   in the morning I will sing of
        your love;
for you are my fortress,
   my refuge in times of trouble.

PSALM 59:16

Blessed are those whose strength is in you,
   who have set their hearts on pilgrimage.
As they pass through the Valley of Baca,
   they make it a place of springs;
   the autumn rains also cover it with pools.
They go from strength to strength,
   till each appears before God in Zion.

PSALM 84:5–7

The LORD is the strength of his people,
a fortress of salvation for his
anointed one.

PSALM 28:8

It is God who arms me with strength
and makes my way perfect.
He makes my feet like the feet of a deer;
he enables me to stand on the heights.

PSALM 18:32–33

The LORD is my strength and my song;
he has become my salvation.
He is my God, and I will praise him,
my father's God, and I will exalt him.

EXODUS 15:2

STRESS

"I will refresh the weary and satisfy the faint," says the LORD Almighty.

JEREMIAH 31:25

This is what the Sovereign LORD, the Holy One of Israel, says:
"In repentance and rest is your salvation,
    in quietness and trust is your strength."

ISAIAH 30:15

Cast your cares on the LORD
    and he will sustain you;
    he will never let the righteous fall.

PSALM 55:22

Do not be anxious about anything, but in everything, by prayer and petition, with thanksgiving, present your requests to God. And the peace of God, which transcends all understanding, will guard your hearts and your minds in Christ Jesus.

PHILIPPIANS 4:6–7

The LORD will be your confidence
    and will keep your foot from being snared.

PROVERBS 3:26

You will keep in perfect peace
him whose mind is steadfast,
because he trust in you.
Trust in the LORD *forever,*
for the LORD, *the* LORD, *is the Rock eternal.*

ISAIAH 26:3–4

Cast all your anxiety on him because he cares for you.

I PETER 5:7

Jesus said, "Come to me, all you who are weary and
burdened, and I will give you rest. Take my yoke
upon you and learn from me, for I am gentle and
humble in heart, and you will find rest for your
souls. For my yoke is easy and my burden is light."

MATTHEW 11:28–30

May the Lord of peace himself give you peace at all times and in every way. The Lord be with all of you.

2 THESSALONIANS 3:16

SUCCESS

Commit to the LORD whatever
you do,
and your plans will succeed.

PROVERBS 16:3

May [God] give you the desire of your heart
and make all your plans succeed.
We will shout for joy when you are victorious
and will lift up our banners in the name of
our God.
May the LORD grant all your requests.

PSALM 20:4–5

You will have success if you are careful to observe
the decrees and laws that the LORD gave Moses for
Israel. Be strong and courageous. Do not be afraid
or discouraged.

1 CHRONICLES 22:13

Plans fail for lack of counsel,
but with many advisers they
succeed.

PROVERBS 15:22

Blessed is the man who fears the LORD,
*   who finds great delight in his commands.*
His children will be mighty in the land;
*   the generation of the upright will be blessed.*
Wealth and riches are in his house,
*   and his righteousness endures forever.*

PSALM 112:1–3

Jehoshaphat said, "Have faith in the LORD your God and you will be upheld; have faith in his prophets and you will be successful."

2 CHRONICLES 20:20

The LORD said, "Do not let this Book of the Law depart from your mouth; meditate on it day and night, so that you may be careful to do everything written in it. Then you will be prosperous and successful. Have I not commanded you? Be strong and courageous. Do not be terrified; do not be discouraged, for the LORD your God will be with you wherever you go."

JOSHUA 1:8–9

TALENTS & GIFTS

We have different gifts, according to the grace given us. If a man's gift is prophesying, let him use it in proportion to his faith. If it is serving, let him serve; if it is teaching, let him teach; if it is encouraging, let him encourage; if it is contributing to the needs of others, let him give generously; if it is leadership, let him govern diligently; if it is showing mercy, let him do it cheerfully.

ROMANS 12:6–8

God's gifts and his call are irrevocable.

ROMANS 11:29

A gift opens the way for the giver
and ushers him into the presence of the great.

PROVERBS 18:16

Every good and perfect gift is from above, coming down from the Father of the heavenly lights, who does not change like shifting shadows.

JAMES 1:17

Each man has his own gift from God; one has this gift, another has that.

I CORINTHIANS 7:7

There are different kinds of gifts, but the same Spirit. There are different kinds of service, but the same Lord. There are different kinds of working, but the same God works all of them in all men. Now to each one the manifestation of the Spirit is given for the common good.

I CORINTHIANS 12:4–7

Each one should use whatever gift he has received to serve others, faithfully administering God's grace in its various forms. If anyone speaks, he should do it as one speaking the very words of God. If anyone serves, he should do it with the strength God provides, so that in all things God may be praised through Jesus Christ.

I PETER 4:10–11

THANKFULNESS

Thanks be to God for his indescribable gift!

2 CORINTHIANS 9:15

In everything, by prayer and petition, with thanks-giving, present your requests to God. And the peace of God, which transcends all understanding, will guard your hearts and your minds in Christ Jesus.

PHILIPPIANS 4:6–7

Give thanks in all circumstances, for this is God's will for you in Christ Jesus.

I THESSALONIANS 5:18

Since we are receiving a kingdom that cannot be shaken, let us be thankful, and so worship God accept-ably with reverence and awe.

HEBREWS 12:28

Just as you received Christ Jesus as Lord, continue to live in him, rooted and built up in him, strength-ened in the faith as you were taught, and overflow-ing with thankfulness.

COLOSSIANS 2:6–7

Thanks be to God! He gives us the victory through our Lord Jesus Christ.

1 CORINTHIANS 15:57

Let the word of Christ dwell in you richly as you teach and admonish one another with all wisdom, and as you sing psalms, hymns and spiritual songs with gratitude in your hearts to God.

COLOSSIANS 3:16

Let them give thanks to the LORD for his
unfailing love
and his wonderful deeds for men,
for he satisfies the thirsty
and fills the hungry with good things.

PSALM 107:8–9

The LORD is my strength and my shield;
my heart trusts in him, and I am helped.
My heart leaps for joy
and I will give thanks to him in song.

PSALM 28:7

THOUGHTS

The mind of sinful man is death, but the mind controlled by the Spirit is life and peace.

ROMANS 8:6

Whatever is true, whatever is noble, whatever is right, whatever is pure, whatever is lovely, whatever is admirable—if anything is excellent or praise-worthy—think about such things.

PHILIPPIANS 4:8

How precious to me are your thoughts, O God!
    How vast is the sum of them!
Were I to count them,
    they would outnumber the grains of sand.

PSALM 139:17–18

Those who live in accordance with the Spirit have their minds set on what the Spirit desires.

ROMANS 8:5

Be clear minded and self-controlled so that you can pray.

1 PETER 4:7

I the LORD *search the heart*
and examine the mind,
to reward a man according to his conduct,
according to what his deeds deserve.

JEREMIAH 17:10

"My thoughts are not your thoughts,
neither are your ways my ways,"
declares the LORD.

ISAIAH 55:8

The LORD *knows the thoughts of man.*

PSALM 94:11

Holy brothers, who share in the heavenly calling, fix
your thoughts on Jesus, the apostle and high priest
whom we confess.

HEBREWS 3:1

We demolish arguments and every
pretension that sets itself up against
the knowledge of God, and we take
captive every thought to make it
obedient to Christ.

2 CORINTHIANS 10:5

TIME

There is a time for everything,
and a season for every activity under heaven.

ECCLESIASTES 3:1

The wise heart will know the proper time and
procedure.
For there is a proper time and procedure for
every matter.

ECCLESIASTES 8:5–6

I know that everything God does will endure for-
ever; nothing can be added to it and nothing taken
from it. God does it so that men will revere him.

ECCLESIASTES 3:14

You see, at just the right time, when
we were still powerless, Christ died
for the ungodly.

ROMANS 5:6

God has made everything beautiful in its time. He
has also set eternity in the hearts of men; yet they
cannot fathom what God has done from beginning
to end.

ECCLESIASTES 3:11

There will be a time for every activity,
  a time for every deed.

ECCLESIASTES 3:17

My times are in your hands.

PSALM 31:15

A thousand years in your sight, O LORD,
  are like a day that has just gone by,
  or like a watch in the night.

PSALM 90:4

Do not forget this one thing, dear friends: With the Lord a day is like a thousand years, and a thousand years are like a day.

2 PETER 3:8

As God's fellow workers we urge you not to receive God's grace in vain. For he says,

"In the time of my favor I heard you,
  and in the day of salvation I helped you."

I tell you, now is the time of God's favor, now is the day of salvation.

2 CORINTHIANS 6:1–2

TRIALS

The Lord knows how to rescue godly
men from trials.

2 PETER 2:9

*Do not be surprised at the painful trial you are suffer-
ing, as though something strange were happening to
you. But rejoice that you participate in the sufferings
of Christ, so that you may be overjoyed when his
glory is revealed. If you are insulted because of the
name of Christ, you are blessed, for the Spirit of glory
and of God rests on you.*

I PETER 4:12–14

*Blessed is the man who perseveres under trial,
because when he has stood the test, he will receive
the crown of life that God has promised to those
who love him.*

JAMES 1:12

*When you are in distress and all these things have
happened to you, then in later days you will return
to the LORD your God and obey him. For the LORD
your God is a merciful God; he will not abandon
or destroy you or forget the covenant with your
forefathers, which he confirmed to them by oath.*

DEUTERONOMY 4:30–31

No *temptation has seized you except what is common to man. And God is faithful; he will not let you be tempted beyond what you can bear. But when you are tempted, he will also provide a way out so that you can stand up under it.*

1 CORINTHIANS 10:13

Consider it pure joy, my brothers, whenever you face trials of many kinds, because you know that the testing of your faith develops perseverance.

JAMES 1:2

I consider that our present sufferings are not worth comparing with the glory that will be revealed in us.

ROMANS 8:18

The God of all grace, who called you to his eternal glory in Christ, after you have suffered a little while, will himself restore you and make you strong, firm and steadfast.

1 PETER 5:10

TROUBLE

Jesus said, "Do not let your hearts be troubled.
Trust in God; trust also in me."

JOHN 14:1

You are my hiding place;
    you will protect me from trouble
    and surround me with songs of deliverance.

PSALM 32:7

The LORD is a refuge for the
        oppressed,
    a stronghold in times of trouble.

PSALM 9:9

Praise be to the God and Father of our Lord Jesus
Christ, the Father of compassion and the God of all
comfort, who comforts us in all our troubles, so that
we can comfort those in any trouble with the com-
fort we ourselves have received from God.

2 CORINTHIANS 1:3–4

Our light and momentary troubles
are achieving for us an eternal glory
that far outweighs them all.

2 CORINTHIANS 4:17

"Because he loves me," says the LORD, "I will
rescue him;
I will protect him, for he acknowledges
my name.
He will call upon me, and I will answer him;
I will be with him in trouble,
I will deliver him and honor him."

PSALM 91:14–15

A righteous man may have many troubles,
but the LORD delivers him from them all.

PSALM 34:19

Jesus said, "In this world you will have
trouble. But take heart! I have over-
come the world."

JOHN 16:33

Though I walk in the midst of trouble,
you preserve my life;
you stretch out your hand against the anger
of my foes,
with your right hand you save me.

PSALM 138:7

TRUST

The LORD says,
"Blessed is the man who trusts in the LORD,
　　whose confidence is in him.
He will be like a tree planted by the water
　　that sends out its roots by the stream.
It does not fear when heat comes;
　　its leaves are always green.
It has no worries in a year of drought
　　and never fails to bear fruit."

JEREMIAH 17:7–8

Trust in the LORD with all your heart
　　and lean not on your own understanding;
in all your ways acknowledge him,
　　and he will make your paths straight.

PROVERBS 3:5–6

Trust in the LORD and do good; dwell in the land and enjoy safe pasture.

PSALM 37:3

He who trusts in the LORD will prosper.

PROVERBS 28:25

Those who trust in the LORD are like Mount Zion,
*   which cannot be shaken but endures forever.*
As the mountains surround Jerusalem,
*   so the LORD surrounds his people*
*   both now and forevermore.*

PSALM 125:1–2

Trust in the LORD forever,
    for the LORD, the LORD, is the
        Rock eternal.

ISAIAH 26:4

Blessed is the man
*   who makes the LORD his trust,*
who does not look to the proud,
*   to those who turn aside to false gods.*

PSALM 40:4

Anyone who trusts in [the Lord] will
never be put to shame.

ROMANS 10:11

May the God of hope fill you with all joy and peace as you trust in him, so that you may overflow with hope by the power of the Holy Spirit.

ROMANS 15:13

Fear of man will prove to be a snare, but whoever trusts in the LORD is kept safe.

PROVERBS 29:25

Some trust in chariots and some in horses,
but we trust in the name of the LORD
our God.
They are brought to their knees and fall,
but we rise up and stand firm.

PSALM 20:7–8

He who dwells in the shelter of the Most High
will rest in the shadow of the Almighty.
I will say of the LORD, "He is my refuge and
my fortress,
my God, in whom I trust."

PSALM 91:1–2

Many are the woes of the wicked,
but the LORD's unfailing love
surrounds the man who trusts
in him.

PSALM 32:10

Whoever gives heed to instruction prospers,
and blessed is he who trusts in the LORD.

PROVERBS 16:20

Those who know your name will trust in you,
for you, LORD, have never forsaken those who
seek you.

PSALM 9:10

It is better to take refuge in the LORD
than to trust in man.
It is better to take refuge in the LORD
than to trust in princes.

PSALM 118:8–9

Truth

Buy the truth and do not sell it;
get wisdom, discipline and understanding.

Proverbs 23:23

Jesus said, "If you hold to my teaching, you are really my disciples. Then you will know the truth, and the truth will set you free."

John 8:31–32

We know that we are children of God, and that the whole world is under the control of the evil one. We know also that the Son of God has come and has given us understanding, so that we may know him who is true. And we are in him who is true—even in his Son Jesus Christ. He is the true God and eternal life.

1 John 5:19–20

Jesus said, "I have much more to say to you, more than you can now bear. But when he, the Spirit of truth, comes, he will guide you into all truth. He will not speak on his own; he will speak only what he hears, and he will tell you what is yet to come."

John 16:12–13

Jesus answered, "I am the way and the truth and the life. No one comes to the Father except through me."

JOHN 14:6

He whose walk is blameless
and who does what is righteous,
who speaks the truth from his heart ...
will never be shaken.

PSALM 15:2, 5

All your words are true;
all your righteous laws are eternal.

PSALM 119:160

Jesus answered, "For this I came into the world, to testify to the truth. Everyone on the side of truth listens to me."

JOHN 18:37

UNDERSTANDING

*My purpose is that they may be encouraged in heart
and united in love, so that they may have the full
riches of complete understanding, in order that they
may know the mystery of God, namely, Christ, in
whom are hidden all the treasures of wisdom and
knowledge.*

COLOSSIANS 2:2–3

*I have more understanding than the elders,
    for I obey your precepts.
I gain understanding from your precepts.*

PSALM 119:100, 104

*It is the spirit in a man,
    the breath of the Almighty, that gives
        him understanding.*

JOB 32:8

*Though it cost all you have, get understanding.
Esteem her, and she will exalt you;
    embrace her, and she will honor you.
She will set a garland of grace on your head
    and present you with a crown of splendor.*

PROVERBS 4:7–9

Blessed is the man who finds wisdom,
  the man who gains understanding,
for she is more profitable than silver
  and yields better returns than gold.
She is more precious than rubies;
  nothing you desire can compare with her.
Long life is in her right hand;
  in her left hand are riches and honor.
Her ways are pleasant ways,
  and all her paths are peace.
She is a tree of life to those who embrace her;
  those who lay hold of her will be blessed.

PROVERBS 3:13–18

Who is wise and understanding among you? Let him show it by his good life, by deeds done in the humility that comes from wisdom.

JAMES 3:13

He who cherishes understanding prospers.

PROVERBS 19:8

UNITY

*May the God who gives endurance and encourage-
ment give you a spirit of unity among yourselves as
you follow Christ Jesus.*

ROMANS 15:5

There is neither Jew nor Greek, slave
nor free, male nor female, for you
are all one in Christ Jesus.

GALATIANS 3:28

*We were all baptized by one Spirit into one body—
whether Jews or Greeks, slave or free—and we were
all given the one Spirit to drink.*

I CORINTHIANS 12:13

As far as it depends on you, live at
peace with everyone.

ROMANS 12:18

*There is one body and one Spirit—just as you were
called to one hope when you were called—one
Lord, one faith, one baptism; one God and Father
of all, who is over all and through all and in all.*

EPHESIANS 4:4–6

Agree with one another so that there may be no divisions among you.

1 CORINTHIANS 1:10

Jesus said, "I pray also for those who will believe in me.... May they be brought to complete unity to let the world know that you sent me."

JOHN 17:20, 23

Make every effort to keep the unity of the Spirit.

EPHESIANS 4:3

Live in harmony with one another.

ROMANS 12:16

Live in harmony with one another; be sympathetic, love as brothers, be compassionate and humble.

1 PETER 3:8

How good and pleasant it is when brothers live together in unity!

PSALM 133:1

UNSELFISHNESS

A generous man will prosper;
    he who refreshes others will himself be
        refreshed.

PROVERBS 11:25

He who is kind to the poor lends to the LORD,
    and he will reward him for what he has done.

PROVERBS 19:17

If you harbor bitter envy and selfish ambition in your hearts, do not boast about it or deny the truth. Such "wisdom" does not come down from heaven but is earthly, unspiritual, of the devil. For where you have envy and selfish ambition, there you find disorder and every evil practice. But the wisdom that comes from heaven is first of all pure; then peace-loving, considerate, submissive, full of mercy and good fruit, impartial and sincere. Peacemakers who sow in peace raise a harvest of righteousness.

JAMES 3:14–18

Jesus said, "Give to the one who asks you, and do not turn away from the one who wants to borrow from you."

MATTHEW 5:42

Do nothing out of selfish ambition or vain conceit, but in humility consider others better than yourselves. Each of you should look not only to your own interests, but also to the interests of others.

PHILIPPIANS 2:3–4

Jesus said, "Watch out! Be on your guard against all kinds of greed; a man's life does not consist in the abundance of his possessions."

LUKE 12:15

Love is patient, love is kind. It does not envy, it does not boast, it is not proud. It is not rude, it is not self-seeking, it is not easily angered, it keeps no record of wrongs.

1 CORINTHIANS 13:4–5

Turn my heart toward your statutes
*   and not toward selfish gain.*
Turn my eyes away from worthless things;
*   preserve my life according to your word.*

PSALM 119:36–37

VALUES

Whatever is true, whatever is noble, whatever is right, whatever is pure, whatever is lovely, whatever is admirable—if anything is excellent or praiseworthy—think about such things.

PHILIPPIANS 4:8

Jesus said, "Do to others as you would have them do to you."

LUKE 6:31

Be careful that you do not forget the LORD your God, failing to observe his commands, his laws and his decrees. . . . Otherwise, when you eat and are satisfied, when you build fine houses and settle down, and when your herds and flocks grow large and your silver and gold increase and all you have is multiplied, then your heart will become proud and you will forget the LORD your God.

DEUTERONOMY 8:11–14

Be careful, and watch yourselves closely so that you do not forget the things your eyes have seen or let them slip from your heart as long as you live. Teach them to your children and to their children after them.

DEUTERONOMY 4:9

By faith Moses, when he had grown up, refused to be known as the son of Pharaoh's daughter. He chose to be mistreated along with the people of God rather than to enjoy the pleasures of sin for a short time. He regarded disgrace for the sake of Christ as of greater value than the treasures of Egypt, because he was looking ahead to his reward.

HEBREWS 11:24–26

Be shepherds of God's flock that is under your care, serving as overseers—not because you must, but because you are willing, as God wants you to be; not greedy for money, but eager to serve; not lording it over those entrusted to you, but being examples to the flock.

1 PETER 5:2–3

Who may ascend the hill of the LORD?
Who may stand in his holy place?
He who has clean hands and a pure heart,
who does not life up his soul to an idol
or swear by what is false.
He will receive blessing from the LORD
and vindication from God his Savior.

PSALM 24:3–5

311

VICTORY

*[God's] commands are not burdensome, for every-
one born of God overcomes the world. This is the
victory that has overcome the world, even our faith.
Who is it that overcomes the world? Only he who
believes that Jesus is the Son of God.*

1 JOHN 5:3–5

**In all these things we are more than
conquerors through him who loved us.**

ROMANS 8:37

*The LORD your God is the one who goes with you
to fight for you against your enemies to give you
victory.*

DEUTERONOMY 20:4

*We will not all sleep, but we will all be changed—
in a flash, in the twinkling of an eye, at the last
trumpet. For the trumpet will sound, the dead will
be raised imperishable, and we will be changed....
Then the saying that is written will come true:
"Death has been swallowed up in victory." ...
Thanks be to God! He gives us the victory through
our Lord Jesus Christ.*

1 CORINTHIANS 15:51–52, 54, 57

Thanks be to God, who always leads us in triumphal procession in Christ.

2 CORINTHIANS 2:14

[The LORD] holds victory in store for the upright.

PROVERBS 2:7

There is no wisdom, no insight, no plan
that can succeed against the LORD.
The horse is made ready for the day of battle,
but victory rests with the LORD.

PROVERBS 21:30–31

With God we will gain the victory,
and he will trample down our enemies.

PSALM 60:12

Jesus said, "In this world you will have trouble. But take heart! I have overcome the world."

JOHN 16:33

WEALTH

Honor the LORD with your wealth,
*   with the firstfruits of all your crops;*
then your barns will be filled to overflowing,
*   and your vats will brim over with new wine.*

Has not God chosen those who are poor in the eyes of the world to be rich in faith and to inherit the kingdom he promised those who love him?

JAMES 2:5

Fear the LORD, you his saints,
*   for those who fear him lack nothing.*
The lions may grow weak and hungry,
*   but those who seek the LORD lack no*
*   good thing.*

PSALM 34:9–10

Remember the LORD your God, for it is he who gives you the ability to produce wealth, and so confirms his covenant, which he swore to your forefathers, as it is today.

DEUTERONOMY 8:18

The blessing of the LORD brings wealth,
*   and he adds no trouble to it.*

PROVERBS 10:22

You still the hunger of those you cherish;
*   their sons have plenty,*
*   and they store up wealth for their children.*

PSALM 17:14

Command those who are rich ... to be generous
and willing to share. In this way they will lay up
treasure for themselves as a firm foundation for the
coming age, so that they may take hold of the life
that is truly life.

I TIMOTHY 6:17–19

Store up for yourselves treasures in heaven.... For
where your treasure is, there your heart will be also.

MATTHEW 6:20–21

Rich and poor have this in common:
The LORD is the maker of them all.

PROVERBS 22:2

WISDOM

Do not forsake wisdom, and she will protect you;
love her, and she will watch over you.
Wisdom is supreme; therefore get wisdom.

PROVERBS 4:6–7

If any of you lacks wisdom, he should ask God, who gives generously to all without finding fault, and it will be given to him.

JAMES 1:5

I guide you in the way of wisdom
and lead you along straight paths.
When you walk, your steps will not be hampered;
when you run, you will not stumble.

PROVERBS 4:11–12

The wisdom that comes from heaven is first of all
pure; then peace-loving, considerate, submissive, full
of mercy and good fruit, impartial and sincere.

JAMES 3:17

Wisdom, like an inheritance, is a good thing
and benefits those who see the sun.

ECCLESIASTES 7:11

My son, if you accept my words
and store up my commands within you,
turning your ear to wisdom
and applying your heart to understanding,
and if you call out for insight
and cry aloud for understanding,
and if you look for it as for silver
and search for it as for hidden treasure,
then you will understand the fear of the LORD
and find the knowledge of God.

PROVERBS 2:1–5

The fear of the LORD *is the beginning of wisdom;*
all who follow his precepts have good
understanding.

PSALM 111:10

Wisdom is sweet to your soul;
if you find it, there is a future
hope for you,
and your hope will not be cut off.

PROVERBS 24:14

WORK

All hard work brings a profit.

PROVERBS 14:23

God is not unjust; he will not forget your work and the love you have shown him as you have helped his people and continue to help them.

HEBREWS 6:10

Stand firm. Let nothing move you. Always give yourselves fully to the work of the Lord, because you know that your labor in the Lord is not in vain.

1 CORINTHIANS 15:58

From the fruit of his lips a man is filled with
        good things
    as surely as the work of his hands rewards him.

PROVERBS 12:14

Jesus said, "Do not work for food that spoils, but for food that endures to eternal life, which the Son of Man will give you. On him God the Father has placed his seal of approval."

JOHN 6:27

Whatever you do, work at it with all your heart, as working for the Lord, not for men, since you know that you will receive an inheritance from the Lord as a reward.

COLOSSIANS 3:23–24

Don't you know that those who work in the temple get their food from the temple, and those who serve at the altar share in what is offered on the altar? In the same way, the Lord has commanded that those who preach the gospel should receive their living from the gospel.

1 CORINTHIANS 9:13–14

*The sluggard craves and gets nothing,
    but the desires of the diligent are fully satisfied.*

PROVERBS 13:4

Lazy hands make a man poor,
    but diligent hands bring wealth.

PROVERBS 10:4

We want to hear from you. Please send your comments about this book to us in care of zreview@zondervan.com. Thank you.

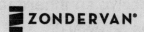